ENERGY SAVING GUIDE

SAVE MONEY ON

HOME HEATING & AIR CONDITIONING
WATER • ELECTRICITY • GAS

Zolton Cohen

P9-APL-657

Publications International, Ltd.

Zolton Cohen is a licensed residential building contractor, syndicated newspaper columnist, and former ASHI-certified home inspector. He lives and works in Kalamazoo, Michigan.

Copyright © 2006 Publications International, Ltd. All rights reserved. This book may not be reproduced or quoted in whole or in part by any means whatsoever without written permission from:

Louis Weber, CEO
Publications International, Ltd.
7373 North Cicero Avenue
Lincolnwood, Illinois 60712

Permission is never granted for commercial purposes.

ISBN-13: 978-1-4127-1328-3

ISBN-10: 1-4127-1328-5

Manufactured in U.S.A.

8 7 6 5 4 3 2 1

Contents

SAVING FUEL IS MONEY IN YOUR POCKET

It's no secret that the price of energy has been rising recently. Anyone who has put gas in a car lately or paid a household utility bill has run into that fact. If you'd like to save money on gas, this book is for you.

The rising price of gas at the pump

Most of the timely tips in these pages will help—whether you drive 1,000 miles a week or never cover that much distance in a month; whether you drive a subcompact, a hybrid, a sports car, or a sport-utility vehicle; whether you agonize daily in rush-hour traffic or seldom stray from uncrowded rural highways.

Much of driving economically is a matter of breaking a few bad habits and substituting some good ones. We've all been warned about "jackrabbit" starts and speeding. Such actions are both dangerous and uneconomical, and yet we see them all the time.

The trouble is, many of us learned to drive at a time when economy was not a high priority and when cars weren't built with thrift in mind. Even the basic scheduled maintenance was mainly for the purpose of boosting performance, not for adding extra miles per gallon.

Americans seldom gave much thought to fuel economy before the Arab Oil Embargo of 1973. The specter of long lines at the gas station, unreliable supply, and fluctuating prices reared again with the fuel crisis of 1979–1980. Those events were wake-up calls, and Detroit and Asian automakers responded with lots of gas-sipping compacts. But by the late 1980s, horsepower and performance were back in vogue.

Average fuel economy for passenger cars, after rising steadily for more than a decade, began to decline by 1989. Cars were getting faster, more powerful, more laden with gadgetry—and gulping more fuel. Americans had evidently decided that a new crisis wasn't going to happen. The popularity of light trucks, notably sport-utility vehicles and pickup trucks, grew quickly in the late '80s when Ford's F-150 pickup became the best-selling vehicle in America, and trendy was spelled S-U-V.

In short, life on the American road was good. We were paying far less for our automotive fun than were motorists in most European countries—just as we had for decades. Adjusted for inflation, motor fuel costs in the late '80s had reached their lowest point since the years just after World War II.

Then, in August 1990, Iraq invaded Kuwait. Within a week, the average price of gasoline shot up more than 16 cents a gallon. A month later, prices stabilized somewhat, though at a level 30 cents higher than before the crisis. Suddenly, government officials issued stern warnings about the need for frugality. Polls suggested that many Americans would return to fuel-sipping cars if gas prices reached $1.40 per gallon. More than half claimed they would do so if prices hit $2.00. Many simply said they were already cutting back on driving.

Of course, the modern automobile was already far more frugal than its elephantine ancestors. The average new passenger car achieved 27.8 miles per gallon in 1990. Sure, that was down from a high of 28.6 mpg in 1988, but it was still far thriftier than the 14.2-mpg average of 1974. Maybe America was on the right track after all.

SUVs and other light trucks

Things were also changing at the high-mileage end of the fuel-consumption spectrum. Gas-sipping imports, which had played a major role in redirecting the industry during the 1970s, weren't quite so thrifty anymore. Japanese automakers were veering away from the subcompact and minicar market in which they'd gained their reputations. Instead, they moved upscale, turning to handsome but thirsty performance and luxury models, such as the Infiniti and Lexus sedans introduced for 1990.

By that time, barely 3 percent of shoppers were driving off in cars that yielded 40 mpg or more. About 30 percent of cars available in 1990 offered more than 30 mpg, but few Americans seemed to want one. This is ironic because gas prices, adjusted for inflation, were startlingly high, by U.S. standards.

From 1980 to 1983, pump prices ranged from the infla-tion-adjusted equivalents of $2.60 a gallon to $2.70 a gal-lon. Of course, the actual gas prices were much lower during those years, so the bite didn't seem as bad.

Adjusted for inflation, pump prices actually declined from 1985 to 1987, and then leveled off (except during the price spike of 1990–1991 caused by Gulf War I) at about $1.30–$1.50 a gallon. Then they dropped to $1.00 (adjusted) per gallon in 1998–1999.

That time period marked a high point in America's love affair with the SUV, which was prized for its practical nature, commanding view of the road, presumed safety, and high-class image. And many SUVs, like many pickups, have the added allure of 4-wheel drive—a system that eats up more gas than 2WD.

SUV sales skyrocketed in the early '90s, and by the end of the decade virtually every automaker that maintained a presence in the United States offered one or more sport-utes—even Porsche. There was an SUV or pickup for every budget, demographic, and attitude.

SUVs seriously hurt the sales of more economical station wagons and fuel-efficient minivans. In addition, SUV popularity encouraged the production of a proliferation of pickup trucks. These vehicles, as well as a flock of imported and domestic luxury sedans, swallowed gas the way a thirsty horse gulps water.

Global trouble, domestic disaster

The terrorist attacks of September 11, 2001, initiated a gradual but steady climb in pump prices, which accelerated after America's spring 2003 invasion of Iraq. The American war machine required massive amounts of gasoline and other fuels, and as with any war, combat costs soon made their way back to the folks at home.

When Congress legislated new fuel economy standards in 2003 for all cars and light trucks sold in the United States, the passenger-car average was a meager 13.5

miles per gallon, while the light truck average was 11.6 mpg. Those low figures made America vulnerable to future gasoline price hikes, but drivers didn't seem to notice. A devastating price spike was just speculation. And anyway, inflation was low, and if the economy wasn't exactly robust, it did seem to be shaking off some of the effects of the 2000–2002 recession.

The $2-per-gallon barrier was shattered in 2004, but prices didn't stop there. Iraqi oil production was crippled by the war, and American demand for gas—360 million gallons every day—continued unabated.

The EPA's city and highway mileage estimates for 2005, which were put together in late 2004, assumed '05 gas prices of $1.90 per gallon for regular and $1.95 for premium.

But in 2005 the per-barrel price for crude oil on the world market jumped to $50, startling economists and other analysts. Pump prices rose. Then came $60 per barrel. Pump prices continued to rise. The average cost of a gallon of gas in the United States at the end of summer 2005 approached $3 a gallon, a figure exceeded in many urban areas. Every oil-producing country save Saudi Arabia was producing at full capacity. We wanted more oil, but it wasn't going to come easily. President Bush authorized use of the nation's strategic oil reserve to help keep pump prices in check. Europe, too, released some of its reserves onto the world market.

At the end of August 2005, Hurricane Katrina devastated the Gulf States and badly damaged oil refineries and port facilities vital to America's fuel interests. Because the disaster prompted oil companies to increase the wholesale gas price charged to station owners, pump prices in the days following Katrina rose by 10, 20, 30 cents, and more, in single leaps. Some stations exploited customers with pump prices closer to $4; in the South, some motorists paid as much as $6 per gallon.

When the federal government declared a prohibition on price gouging, the most egregious pump prices declined. But underground tanks at a few independent stations ran dry, and drivers began to worry that big oil stations might have similar shortfalls. By September 2005, some experts looked to the near future and saw an average pump price of $4 per gallon, perhaps higher.

It's easy to see why interest in fuel economy had nearly evaporated prior to 9/11 and again before the American action in Iraq. Americans felt that at $1.50 per gallon, even $2.00, the pleasure-to-pain ratio was acceptable. At $1.50 per gallon the average driver—who consumes a bit more than 500 gallons each year, traveling just over 10,000 miles—paid about $750 annually. Two-dollar gas took the average over the $1,000 mark—a significant amount, but one that Americans were willing to pay. But $3 per gallon means an annual outlay of $1,500, and if you're already paying more than $3, well, you can do the math for yourself.

Still, it's important to note that gas prices in late 2005, adjusted for inflation, were at about the same level as in the early 1980s, and overall improvements in fuel economy meant that drivers paid nearly 40 percent less to drive a mile than they did 20 years ago.

Gasoline remains a bargain in the United States, particularly relative to the retail cost of premium bottled water and other everyday commodities. For example, a 20-ounce café mocha costs about $3.50, and although it tastes good, it won't get you nearly as far as a gallon (128 fluid ounces) of gas.

Consider, also, that U.S. gas prices are only about half of what is charged in Europe, where drivers and automakers have learned to adjust. Further, U.S. capacity to refine oil, though compromised by Katrina, was not harmed critically. All of us benefit from the social and economic opportunities made possible by gasoline and the American tradition of personal transport. Calm, sensible driving and buying decisions will see you through almost any fuel-economy challenge.

Getting the best gas mileage

The first two chapters of this book explain how you can get the best fuel economy from your present vehicle, whether an economy car, a luxury sedan, a 4WD SUV, or a pickup. This means taking a look at how you drive, where you drive, and how you use options and accessories that drain away more fuel than many of us realize.

These chapters also describe the essential steps of basic preventive maintenance, some of which you can do yourself. Not only does such maintenance help eke out more miles per gallon, it extends the life of your car, so you're saving money over the long haul as well as the short term. In addition, scheduled maintenance helps make sure your engine is emitting its minimal potential of pollutants into our precious atmosphere.

So, get started on the road to MMPG (more miles per gallon). Then, maybe we can look forward to the time when people start to boast about their gas mileage as much as their 0-60 mph times.

Saving energy at home

The last five chapters of this book explain how you can get the best use of the energy in your home and thereby also save money.

While there's not much anyone can do about what utility companies charge for the energy they provide, there are quite a few things each one of us can do in our homes to control that use of energy—and therefore the monthly utility bills.

This section of the book helps you understand where the energy you use in your home goes, how some of it is wasted, and how you can make the energy you purchase work harder for your benefit. These suggestions will help you reduce your consumption of energy. The goals are to change the way you think about energy use and conserva-tion and to help you make choices that will result in a posi-tive and personal, as well as environmental, impact.

Many of the energy-saving techniques in these chapters do not involve extra money or time. Simple changes of habit or lifestyle due to increased awareness of energy issues can yield savings.

"Live Efficiently" will cover ways you can modify some of the things you do—and the way you live in your house—in order to conserve energy.

"Increase Energy Efficiency" offers suggestions about energy efficiency that might require a few skills to imple-ment—either for free or with a small investment in materi-als and time.

"Get Your Hands Dirty" contains valuable information about how a higher level of involvement through air sealing, insulation, and weather stripping can handsomely reward someone willing to do the work or to have it done professionally.

"Make Improvements Around the House" is a discussion of how upgrading some of the equipment in your home—furnaces, boilers, air-conditioning systems, appliances—can have a big effect on your energy bill, and why investing in some of the new technology on the market makes sense. It will give you insight into some of the recent energy-saving developments in the fields of heating, air-conditioning, and window replacement. If nothing else, the information will provide you with terminology and an understanding that will help you talk knowledgeably with a contractor doing work on your home.

"Consider Whole House Issues" deals with some health and safety issues that may come into play as you work to weatherize. It answers the question of whether or not you can make a house "too airtight." Also included is information about ice dam formation on rooftops in the winter: a symptom of an energy-inefficient home.

As you read this book you will realize that the benefits of intelligent, reduced use of energy are manifold. Not only can you put your utility bills on a diet, but you can also make an impact on the environment in terms of air quality and water conservation. The less energy you use, the less energy needs to be generated; thus fewer power plants need to be built and the less they need to run. Our country's dependence on foreign oil supplies can be cut back, and we can stretch existing supplies of coal, oil, and natural gas so that our children and grandchildren can live their lives in comfort similar to our own.

It might seem that some of the tiny, incremental steps toward energy conservation suggested in these pages don't mean much in the overall scheme of things. But as a Chinese proverb tells us, "A journey of a thousand miles begins with a single step." All those individual steps add up over time. Multiplied by the millions of homes in this country, even a slight reduction in personal energy-usage habits can result in a significant conservation of energy supplies.

So, too, can the multiple small steps toward energy conservation you take in your own home result in lower energy bills. While some of the tips in these chapters might seem inconsequential, added together they can have a surprising—and pleasing—effect on the bottom line of your monthly utility bill. Multiplied over the course of a year, your "thousand steps" can help you achieve better energy efficiency. And that can add up to real savings—in more ways than one.

THINK ECONOMICALLY

Small changes can result in substantial savings in gas and money. Some of the best fuel-saving techniques are also the easiest:

- **Start by determining whether it's necessary to drive.**

- **If it is, think about your most efficient route.**

- **Prepare and maintain your car to get the best mileage.**

IS THAT DRIVE NECESSARY?

Explore alternative forms of transportation

In a society that values private transportation, going without a car may seem like heresy. Yet surprising numbers of people do exactly that—especially those who live in urban areas.

Walking, after all, is excellent exercise and costs absolutely nothing.

Most cities have better bus service than many nonriders may realize. And in some urban areas, commuter rail service efficiently transports thousands of people to and from work each day. You'll give up some travel-time flexibility, but the duration of your commute may shrink, and you'll be free from the burden of locating and paying for in-town parking.

Lifelong rush-hour motorists may be amazed to discover how relaxing it can be to sit back on the bus or commuter train and read or doze. Train and bus schedules are readily available, usually online. If you can't see giving up the car commute entirely, what about taking mass transit once or twice per week?

Don't overlook the possibility of riding a bicycle instead of traveling by car. It's fine exercise. You won't have parking hassles. Many cities have bike lanes. And in rush-hour congestion, you may find that the maneuverability of a bike

What Factors Establish the Price of Gas

The price of gas at the pump will differ from station to station. It will also vary from one region of the country to another. Both ranges are due to many variables, but all have to with the following factors: the cost of crude oil, refining, distribution and marketing, and, of course, taxes (both federal and state). In general, the cost of crude oil will constitute nearly half of the price at the pump, the cost of refining nearly one fifth, the cost of distribution and marketing about one tenth, and taxes more than one quarter. Supply and demand, state taxes, and transport distances to refineries may vary greatly according to region. While all four factors contribute to the price of retail gas, the number of variables is incalculable.

allows you to travel more quickly than by car. Approach this alternative with due caution, of course. The right bike, proper safety attire, and an alert mindset are essential.

A moped or motorcycle won't free you from all of the costs and burdens of motorized travel, but they afford many of the same advantages as a bicycle, with the obvious ability to go faster and cover longer distances.

The online advantage

Finding the lowest gas prices in your area is just a mouse-click away. Several Web sites allow you to type in your zip code and view a roster of pump prices for your region. Just go to your search engine and type in "gas prices."

The Web also offers a universe of service options from the comfort of your home. Shop online instead of driving to the mall. Bank online instead of idling in a drive-up bank-window line. Conduct research via the Web instead of driving to the library. You can order videos, have digital photos developed, and even buy a car online.

Vacation sensibly

Look into holiday spots where the need to drive after you arrive is minimal or nonexistent. Consider a self-contained resort where you'll enjoy a break from the stress of traffic congestion. Visit an exciting big city, where restaurants, shopping, entertainment, and museums are within walking distance.

If you prefer to take a driving vacation, do a little research on attractions close to home. You might have overlooked some great destinations.

Whether traveling near or far, start out when traffic is light. Plan meals and rest stops to coincide with peak traffic times in the area. There's no point in feeling like a commuter when you're on vacation.

Car pool

Share the ride, share the costs. Talk with neighbors and coworkers about car-pool opportunities, even for just a couple days per week. You'll save on gas, parking, and wear and tear on your car since you will skip a day or two of stop-and-go driving.

You'll save time, too. Many highway systems around big cities have car-pool lanes, otherwise known as High Occupancy Vehicle (HOV) lanes, dedicated to vehicles carrying more than one occupant. While the regular lanes are clogged with crawling peak-travel-time traffic, the HOV lanes are often flowing freely. In rural areas, lots may be set aside as car-pool gathering points near a freeway on-ramp.

PLAN YOUR ROUTE

Become your own traffic manager

Planning and modifying where you drive and how you get there can make a big difference in the number of times you have to stop for fuel every week.

What's the point of leaving the house half a dozen times in the course of a day when a little planning will allow you to do everything in one or two trips?

Particularly in winter, short trips are hard on an engine, which might never fully warm up. Cold engines guzzle a lot more fuel than properly warmed engines.

Drive to the farthest locale first, so the engine completely warms up before you shut it off. Stop-and-go driving with a cold engine puts an even greater strain on its parts.

Drivers who use their cars for business can also learn to plan their trips for the shortest total distance and greatest efficiency, as can families planning medical appointments and school activities.

The multi-car family advantage

Survey the vehicles available to you, and choose the one that's most fuel efficient. Why take the luxury car or heavy-weight SUV on a quick trek to the supermarket when you could slip into your subcompact instead?

Another way to save fuel is to take the vehicle that's been driven most recently. As stated above, engines are grossly inefficient when cold. Start-ups are hard on the car and drastically cut into fuel mileage for the first few miles—all the more so in cold weather. If you have at your disposal a vehicle whose engine isn't stone-cold, consider that one for your errand.

Investigate alternative routes

It's easy to get into a rut, taking the same route day after day, never pondering an alternative that might prove more economical—and even more pleasant.

Experimenting pays. It doesn't hurt to study a map of the region you travel daily. Consider the number of stoplights along the way and the extent of traffic jams and slowdowns.

Use your odometer to measure the distance covered by each route.

Sometimes, it's even wise to travel a little farther if that helps you avoid excess traffic. Whenever feasible, choose highway travel rather than city routes. Avoid routes that pass through school zones or follow school bus pickup points, which often require slowing to an uneconomical speed and perhaps stopping frequently.

Drive when others are not driving

Plan your time so you're traveling when most other people are not. Ask your employer about flexible work hours that keep you out of the morning and evening rush. Run errands at midday rather than 8:00 A.M. or 4:30 P.M.

Off-peak travel saves fuel and aggravation. Leave rush hours to those who have no choice in the matter.

Drive where others are not driving

In the city, look for through streets with a minimum of stoplights. You might think you're saving time by darting down side streets and alleys in rush hour, but you're more likely wasting fuel from all the start-and-stop motion.

Tune into local radio and TV programs for up-to-the-minute reports on traffic conditions and accidents. Staying tuned is most vital in bad weather.

Weather makes a difference

Naturally, you can't change the weather, but the fact is that you'll burn considerably less fuel driving when the temperature is 70 degrees versus 20 degrees. In cold weather, try to travel in daylight rather than at night when it's chillier.

Wind also makes a big difference. A strong headwind, even a crosswind, cuts mileage drastically, as your engine fights its way forward. A tailwind can do the opposite.

Heavy rain and snow also hurt gas mileage, as well as making the travel experience less pleasant. So if you must drive in stormy weather, slow down when the wind is not at your back.

Dress right

Running the heat burns more fuel. Keep that coat zipped and turn the heater blower down a notch or two.

In warm weather, dress lightly to avoid using the air conditioner until absolutely necessary. Even opening the windows creates aerodynamic drag, so proper dress can help you regulate your body temperature to stay comfortable and save fuel.

PREPARE YOUR VEHICLE

Tires: A vital consideration

Proper tire inflation is critical to fuel economy, and to safety.

Underinflated tires cause vehicle drag and increase fuel consumption. They also compromise handling ability in turns and in emergency maneuvers. They increase stopping distances and decrease control during braking. Under-inflation puts undue stress on tire sidewalls and also causes rolling tires to build and retain heat rapidly. Stress and heat are prime contributors to tire failure, including blowouts at high speed. Underinflated tires also wear down more quickly.

Properly inflated tires are harder and roll more easily. That helps fuel economy and improves tire life. It allows the treads to grip well in all conditions, including rain and snow. And properly inflated tires are able to work with your vehicle's suspension to provide maximum handling, steering, and braking ability.

An estimated four out of ten vehicles on the road have at least one underinflated tire. Pressure that's 3 pounds per square inch (psi) below the recommended reading may reduce gas mileage by 1.5 percent. Some experts suggest even greater decreases. The Environmental Protection Agency warns that running tires at 20 psi or lower can easily cost you a full mile per gallon.

Proper tire inflation

Tires can naturally lose up to 1 psi every 30 days, and they will lose pressure more quickly in cold weather. Because cooler air is more dense, pressure drops by about 1 psi for every 10 degrees. A tire inflated to 30 psi at 70 degrees, for example, could drop as low as 26 psi at the freezing point.

The recommended tire pressure is displayed in your vehicle, typically on a sticker inside the glove box door or on one of the doorposts. It's also in your owner's manual. Many vehicles are available with a choice of tire sizes, and each size may have its own recommended inflation pressure.

Match the tire size as listed on the tire sidewall with that on the sticker or in the owner's manual. Note that the inflation number listed on the tire sidewall itself shows the maximum inflation, not the optimal pressure as determined by the tire maker and the manufacturer of your vehicle.

Checking tire inflation

Check inflation when the tires are cool. That means they have been driven less than a mile or so. Air expands inside a warm tire, which will give you a false reading.

Tire pressure should be checked at least every 30 days. A tire gauge is the old standby. But federal regulations require that by 2008 all new cars, SUVs, minivans, and pickup trucks be equipped with an underinflation warning system. Sensors will monitor tire pressure, and if it falls 25 percent below the recommended inflation, a yellow warning light on the dashboard will illuminate.

The system will save an estimated 120 lives and prevent 8,400 injuries annually, according to the National Highway Traffic Safety Administration. NHTSA estimates it will also save drivers up to $35 annually because of longer tread life and decreased fuel costs. Select 2004 and 2005 models already have such a system. For the 2006 model year, 20 percent of new vehicles must have the system, with 70 percent for 2007, and 100 percent for 2008.

Fuel economy varies with tire type

Those all-terrain or off-road tires with their knobby tread look rough and ready and are designed to get you through rocks and mud. They are not designed to promote high gas mileage.

All-season tires produce less friction and therefore roll more freely to the benefit of fuel economy. They're gener-

ally lighter than all-terrain or off-road tires, and less
weight means better fuel economy. They also ride more
quietly, handle better, and wear longer.

Don't carry more than you need

Keep the car as light as reasonably possible. For each
100 pounds of extra weight, gas mileage is reduced by as
much as 4 percent. Limit the everyday items in your trunk
or cargo area to the bare necessities, which should include
some emergency items, such as a small jug of water, a
flashlight, and a few tools.

Don't haul around what you won't be using. Leave the
golf clubs at home until you head for the links. Not only
does extra bulk add fuel-gulping weight, but it can also
upset your vehicle's normal weight distribution. That will
impair handling and can even rob a front-wheel-drive car
of valuable traction. If you must carry heavy items, try to
put only a few of them inside the car at a time.

Remove that rack

Wind drag increases fuel consumption. Get rid of anything
that disturbs the smooth flow of air over your vehicle's
surface. Most roof racks have removable cross members,
and some racks can be removed altogether; take off your
car's rack if it isn't in use. When you do need to carry
something on the roof, keep it light and small—both for
fuel-saving aero-dynamics and to avoid the risk of a top-
heavy weight imbalance.

That grille bar and those running boards may make
your SUV look rugged, but they also add weight and drag.
And that bolt-on trunk-lid spoiler that makes you feel fast

and furious? It's designed to harness the wind and press your car to the pavement at high speeds. The result is better grip on the road, but this "downforce" is actually artificial weight that hurts fuel economy. Worse, unless you are a racing technician versed in aerodynamics, chances are excellent that your spoiler isn't doing anything more than adding wind drag and weight. That's costing you at the pump, too.

Retain that tailgate

Some pickup-truck drivers take it as an article of faith that they're saving fuel by driving with the tailgate down, or removed, or replaced by a mesh fabric or metal gate. False.

Aerodynamic studies show a pickup truck is most fuel efficient with its tailgate up. It seems the upright tailgate causes air flowing over the roof of the cab to collect as a stagnant "dome" in the cargo bed. As speed builds, this dome, which tapers in a teardrop shape near the tailgate, acts as an aerodynamic ramp that forces airflow over the tailgate, to the benefit of fuel efficiency.

Disrupt this flow by dropping or removing the tailgate, and air coming over the cab is left to swirl around in the cargo bed, degrading the truck's aerodynamics and hurting fuel economy.

MAINTAIN YOUR VEHICLE

Poor maintenance means poor mileage

Even simple things like dirty air filters, excessive exhaust emissions, and underinflated tires can combine to reduce fuel economy by as much as 25 percent.

Routine maintenance on a modern vehicle is relatively easy. Electronics and computerized systems mean there's less to tune and that intervals between servicing are surprisingly longer. For example, spark plugs that used to need changing every 10,000 miles now can go 30,000 or even 50,000 miles before needing to be changed.

> **EPA**
> In July 1970, the White House and Congress established the U.S. Environmental Protection Agency (EPA) to protect the health and the environment of Americans. The EPA employs 18,000 people throughout the United States and has more than a dozen labs working on developing a cleaner, healthier environment. One of its major concerns is how efficiently fuel is used and exhausted in vehicles.

Regular maintenance pays off every day

Cars that start quickly, run smoothly, and are in good mechanical condition get the best gas mileage. Whatever cuts into performance hurts economy. Scheduled maintenance also helps make parts last longer, so you save money two ways: today in economy, tomorrow in reduced repair costs.

A tune-up can boost fuel economy up to 10 percent, says the Environmental Protection Agency (EPA). On modern fuel-injected cars equipped with computer-controlled powertrain systems, there's actually little to "tune up." Basically, today's tune-up means replacing the spark plugs, although it's also important to perform the kind of preventive maintenance described later in this section.

Follow the schedule

Your owner's manual will likely list two maintenance schedules: one for "ordinary" driving; the other for "severe" or "heavy-duty" use. Each has its own maintenance program and lists the systems to be checked and the work to be done based on both mileage and time elapsed between servicing.

Even if you don't tow a trailer or drive in dusty conditions, your "ordinary" use can fall into the heavy-duty category if you live in a region subject to very hot or very cold temperatures. Even driving your vehicle on frequent short trips counts as heavy-duty use.

When in doubt, err toward the stricter maintenance schedule. It'll pay off in fuel savings weekly, and in long-term reliability.

Emissions and fuel economy

Exhaust emissions should be checked at least yearly for older vehicles. The lower a car's tailpipe emissions, the more efficiently its engine is operating.

Bringing your car's emissions down to within specifications can improve gas mileage as much as 15 percent. And your engine will last longer, too. The oxygen sensor is a key part of your emissions system, and some estimates suggest that a faulty oxygen sensor can reduce fuel economy by as much as 40 percent.

Under federal law, most emissions controls are covered by the factory warranty for 5 years or 50,000 miles. And some emissions-related repairs may be covered at no cost to you.

Look, listen, and sniff

Be alert for anything odd. Open the hood and look for loose wires or hoses. Check fluid levels regularly, as described later in this section. Be aware of any sudden drop in fuel economy or a curious odor. Monitor the coolant-temperature gauge, if your vehicle has one. As we'll see, running too cold costs fuel. Take note of any pinging or odd noises, hard starting, or significant loss of power.

SIMPLE DO-IT-YOURSELF GAS-SAVING MAINTENANCE

Stay in tune with your car

For economy's sake, you should know a little something about what's going on under the hood. Though undeniably complex and computerized, the principles of engine operation haven't changed as much over the years as many believe. Even if you don't do the work yourself, a bit of knowledge goes a long way when communicating with your mechanic and in making sure all the scheduled maintenance gets done.

A little knowledge is a good thing

We're not talking manuals with instructions on replacing your transmission. And, for better or worse, modern vehicles don't afford too many do-it-yourself opportunities.

But there are many books, brochures, and videotapes that can help you get some basic insight into the purpose and workings of your vehicle. Examine these materials before you buy, however, and be sure they are aimed at your skill level and are current with the systems on your vehicle.

Don't overlook the automaker's shop manual for your car. Though written primarily with factory-authorized mechanics in mind, it contains plenty of useful information to guide the experienced do-it-yourselfer.

Check and change the oil regularly

Oil is the lifeblood of your vehicle's engine, and maintaining proper oil levels and fresh oil will help keep your engine healthy and operating most efficiently. That leads to gas savings.

Check the level on the dipstick weekly. The oil should be checked with the engine turned off. The best time to get an accurate reading is when the engine is cold and the oil is pooled in the oil pan rather than dispersed throughout the engine's oil passages.

Always use the correct oil viscosity, as outlined in your owner's manual. The viscosity is described as 5W30 or 10W40, for example, and is a measurement of the oil blend's ability to do its job within a particular range of conditions and temperatures.

Using the incorrect viscosity can lower fuel economy by up to 2 percent.

Any oil that carries an American Petroleum Institute (API) certification is appropriate. The API also monitors for friction-reducing additives and applies the term "Energy Conserving" to its performance symbol on motor oils that meet this standard.

Some synthetic motor oils are advertised as promoting fuel savings, though the advantage is generally negligible compared to simply changing your oil and filter regularly. Some tests have shown that synthetic oils result in slightly improved fuel economy, though their primary purpose is for use in high-performance engines as part of the total per-formance package. Synthetic oils are quite a bit more expensive than regular oil.

It's become fashionable to change your engine's oil and oil filter every 3,000 miles. It won't hurt to keep to that schedule, though evidence that it's a bit of overkill is in every owner's manual. Most manufacturers specify 15,000 miles or so between oil changes. They built the engine and should know what it needs to stay in top shape.

Some vehicles even have an oil-life monitor that will announce via a dashboard light when an oil change is necessary. This keeps track of how the vehicle is driven between oil changes and recommends when the oil should be changed.

If the manufacturer's oil-change schedule is outlined in the owner's manual or announced on a dashboard light, we recommend that you follow it.

Change the air filter

Some experts say not to expect a huge mileage boost from keeping your engine's air filter fresh; others say a clogged air filter can reduce gas mileage by as much as 10 percent.

In any case, changing an air filter is a simple task you can perform, and a properly operating air filter is essential for keeping the engine clean inside. A clogged or really dirty air filter cuts off air to the engine, and there's no doubt that hurts performance and fuel economy.

The cooling system

An engine that runs too cool or too hot may waste 10 to 15 percent of the fuel you put into your gas tank. Your engine's operating temperature is governed primarily by the coolant fluid and the engine's thermostat.

Coolant is a blend of antifreeze and water that helps maintain proper engine temperature in both hot and cold weather conditions. The proper coolant blend is usually a 50-50 mix of antifreeze and water. The level should be maintained as indicated on the underhood reservoir, and the coolant should look clean.

A malfunctioning thermostat might stick open, which lengthens engine warm-up time and lowers the operating temperature, both of which hamper gas mileage. It could also stick in the closed position, which can cause the engine to overheat. Watch your dashboard coolant temperature gauge as a guide. Even if your car has no gauge but a warning light, one way to discover a malfunctioning thermostat is to pay attention to your car's heater. If it isn't delivering warm air within five minutes, even in freezing weather, get that thermostat checked.

Check belt tensions

Belts that drive the air conditioner, water pump, and power-steering pump must be tight enough not to slip, but

not so tight as to bind. A rule of thumb used to suggest
that belts needed a half-inch of slack, but some of today's
engines are more delicate. Their belts must be checked by
following the manual's instructions exactly, possibly using
a measuring instrument to get tension exactly right. In any
case, don't forget to shut off the engine before putting your
hand anywhere near a belt!

Inspect the battery

Batteries used to demand water periodically, but most of
today's batteries are maintenance-free. What you can still
do is inspect the cable terminals for corrosion and clean-
liness. That can make the difference between getting an
engine to start quickly and wasting gas while the engine
cranks over too slowly—or not at all.

An engine block heater

Motorists in the south may never give a moment's thought
to such a device, but people in the north know this one
well. Many of their cars have a little telltale plug sticking
out of the grille. Connect it to ordinary house current
and the crankcase stays warm overnight. Not only does
the engine turn more freely in the morning, but it also
warms up faster and wastes less fuel during that crucial
period.

Pay attention to the brakes

Take note of suspicious symptoms. A dragging brake is not
only dangerous but can also drag gas mileage down with
every rotation. Brake maintenance is best left to an experienced mechanic. However, if you feel comfortable putting

a corner of your car on a jack, as though you're changing a tire, give the wheel a spin to see if anything seems to be dragging. If it is, contact your mechanic. And make sure the parking brake is never left engaged when you start the car.

Wheel alignment and tire balance

Professional equipment is needed to check these, but a misaligned front end or unbalanced tire can rob plenty of mileage.

Is the car pulling to the side? Chances are a realignment is needed. Unless front wheels are pointing ahead properly, the tires might scrub against the pavement and steal fuel by straining the engine. Vibration at various road speeds suggests the need for balancing. An unbalanced tire also soaks up excess gas.

Promises, promises

If there really were a device that could be added to an engine to yield 100 miles per gallon, it would be front-page news.

Gimmicks claiming to boost gas mileage—a fluid or a gadget of some sort—pop out of the woodwork whenever fuel supply or fuel costs become an issue. These tend to bear a startling resemblance to the "miracle cures" promised by medical charlatans.

The EPA has evaluated more than 100 such "amazing devices" over the years. A half-dozen produced a "statistically significant increase in fuel economy," and a couple of others did so only by increasing emissions levels. Recall the basic money-saving maxim: If it sounds too good to be true, it is.

Be especially wary of extravagant claims for phenomenal mileage, enhanced power, revived performance, and reduced emissions—often all at the same time.

In addition to the questionable fuel and oil additives that promise miraculous mileage, many other additives are produced by reputable companies and sold at auto parts stores. Useful? Depends on who you ask.

Some experts steer clear of chemicals completely. Others allow that the occasional can of fuel-injector cleaner in the tank might help keep the injectors clean. Gas-tank additives can also absorb water that comes in with the latest fillup. Neither result has a direct effect on mileage, however. Basically, a car that's filled with high-quality brands of gasoline and oil shouldn't need any additives to keep it running properly.

DRIVE ECONOMICALLY

Good drivers are smooth drivers, and smooth driving saves fuel. Even minor adjustments in how you drive can result in substantial savings in gas and money.

- **Put yourself in a fuel-saving frame of mind.**

- **Smart driving saves gas.**

- **Choose and use accessories wisely.**

YOU ARE IN CONTROL

Mind over mpg
We tend to allow our emotions to affect our driving. Whether you are elated or angry, calm down before getting behind the wheel.

Emotionally intense drivers are a lot more likely to engage in fuel-wasting (and dangerous) acts: gunning the engine, spinning the wheels, and worse.

Remote starters waste gas
Willing to sacrifice a few minutes of personal comfort to save some gas? Ignore that remote starter.

Remote ignition starters allow you to start your vehicle with the press of a keyfob button while still in the climate-controlled comfort of your home. The vehicle idles with the heater or air conditioner running, and you step into a warm or chilled interior. But an idling car that is running the air-conditioning is needlessly gulping down gas .

The alternative is to bring the vehicle's interior to your desired temperature as you drive, which takes only a few minutes and makes better use of the fuel you're burning.

Remote starters have been available through the after-market for years and recently have been offered as factory-installed options on some new cars. You'll have to judge for yourself whether a few minutes of personal discomfort balances the savings in fuel and the extra exhaust emissions associated with the use of a remote starter.

Warm It on the Run

The modern engine doesn't need long warm-up periods, and idling until it warms up wastes gas—an idling engine gets zero mpg, remember—and is mechanically inefficient, too.

When your vehicle has been sitting for more than a few hours, especially in cold weather, simply start off slowly, without gunning the engine or zipping up to highway speeds. This circulates the vehicle's fluids and loosens up the mechanical components more efficiently than idling in place, and it actually warms the car more quickly.

FILL 'ER UP

Fill the tank only when needed

No point stopping for gas when there's still plenty in the tank. Let it get down to about one-quarter full. Extra stops waste time, and keeping more fuel than needed in the tank adds unwanted weight to your vehicle. A gallon of gas weighs roughly 6 pounds, and the more weight you haul around, the more fuel you'll burn.

Note that there are important exceptions to this rule. During extremely cold weather, keeping the tank near full minimizes the amount of condensation, or water, that can form in the tank. Excess condensation can promote fuel-line freeze and other problems.

Additional exceptions depend on your personal travel patterns. If you regularly drive long distances, at odd hours, in desolate conditions, or in hazardous weather, it's in your interest to keep a generous supply of gas in the tank. Plan for the unexpected.

Buy gas on cool mornings

Liquids expand when warm, and that includes gasoline. So you actually get a bit more for the same amount of cash by buying gas when it's most dense, even though the pump shows the same total.

Gas up along the way

As a rule, there's no point driving out of your way or making a special trip just to save a few cents per gallon. Make the service-station stop part of your regular route.

The exception is during periods of rapid price hikes. Then the difference could amount to more than pennies. So pay attention to current prices in your area, and take note of the stations that offer the most competitive prices.

Gasoline octane ratings

The brand name of the fuel is of no importance to your engine. But the correct octane rating is vital.

Octane has nothing to do with a gasoline's quality. The octane figure indicates a fuel's resistance to "knocking." That's the metallic pinging sound you may sometimes hear when accelerating rapidly or lugging up a hill. Knock may be accompanied by run-on, or dieseling, in which your engine continues to turn over or sputter after you've switched off the ignition. Severe knocking or run-on, over an extended period, can damage engine parts.

There's no advantage in using a higher octane than is necessary to prevent knocking. In fact, today's cars have computerized controls designed to adjust ignition timing and other engine functions to keep knocking in check, so unless you hear something abnormal, you are probably using the right octane level for your car.

What's the correct octane for your vehicle?

Only a small percentage of vehicles require premium fuel. These automobiles are usually sport or luxury vehicles with high-performance engines, and those vehicles with turbo-charged or supercharged gasoline engines.

Regular-grade gas is usually rated at 87 octane, mid-grade at 89 octane, and premium at 91 or above. The higher the altitude above sea level, the lower the octane requirement. You'll see this reflected on the pump: at high altitudes, octane numbers are lower by one or two digits for the same grade of gas available at lower altitudes. Generally, the hotter the air temperature or the lower the humidity, the greater the octane requirement.

It's essential to consult your owner's manual to find out the proper octane level for your vehicle. (Some auto manufacturers also post the octane requirement on a sticker inside the fuel-filler door.)

Note that your owner's manual may list a particular octane level as "recommended" or "required." The "recommended" octane, usually midgrade or premium, is the one you should choose for "best" performance. The manual will state this. Your car will run fine if you choose not to follow that recommendation, and you'll be hard-pressed to notice the few horsepowers sacrificed to the lower octane. If a particular octane level is "required," however, use it.

As vehicles accumulate miles, their octane requirement can increase because of the buildup of combustion-chamber deposits. This continues until a stable level is reached, typically after about 15,000 miles. The stabilized octane requirement may be 3 to 6 numbers higher than when the car was new. Premium or midgrade fuel may be advisable to prevent knocking.

At the gas pump, a label on the pump shows the octane ratings available at that station. The higher the octane, the more you'll pay. Use the correct octane, and save.

FUEL-EFFICIENT DRIVING

Easy does it

Accelerate no more forcefully than needed to mesh smoothly into traffic. Racing up to cruising speed may make you feel like Jeff Gordon, but it'll quickly drain your wallet.

Fuel consumption is directly related to how hard the engine is working. Ask it to race away from a stop rather than accelerate sensibly, and you'll be visiting the gas station all too frequently. Guaranteed. Ask it to barge up a steep grade rather than feathering the throttle just enough to sustain momentum, and you'll watch the needle on your gas gauge move too quickly toward "E."

Even jabbing the accelerator during passing maneuvers or lane changes eats away at fuel economy. On the highway, zooming up to the traffic ahead, then having to hit your brakes, is a fuel-wasting exercise and a sure sign of an impatient driver. The best drivers are smooth and efficient in every move they make.

Lose traction, lose fuel

Even if you're not trying to race away from a stop, you may find your tires slipping, especially on wet or gravel surfaces. Each time a tire slips, whatever the cause, you're losing gas mileage as well as endangering yourself. Take care when starting off on slippery or unpaved roads. Slow down on rough pavement.

RPM and MPG

An engine's workload is determined by how fast the crankshaft is turning. The crankshaft transmits engine power to the transmission and then to the wheels, and crankshaft speed is measured in revolutions per minute, as indicated on a tachometer.

A manual transmission gives the driver full control over rpm because the driver can make the engine speed up or slow down via gear selection. The lower the gear, the higher the rpm. The higher the rpm, the more torque the engine is producing, and the more fuel it is using. Automatic transmissions take some of this control out of the driver's hands, but they, too, can be manipulated to maximize fuel efficiency.

Shift smartly

With a manual gearbox, shift into the upper gears quickly. Optimal shift points vary, depending on the engine/gearing combination, but for best economy you might need to shift to second by about 15 mph, and reach top gear by the time you're traveling 30–35 mph.

Rule of thumb: If the engine is revving faster than necessary to sustain an even road speed, move to the next higher gear. Downshifting follows a similar standard. If the gas pedal has to stay close to the floor to maintain speed, you probably belong in the next lower gear. "Lugging" in too high a gear isn't good for the engine or your finances.

Take advantage of the upshift light

If your manual-transmission car has an upshift indicator, use it as a guide. Using signals from the engine, transmission, and accelerator pedal, the indicator tells you exactly when to upshift to maintain greatest efficiency, and thus top economy.

When the engine speed is high compared to the position of the accelerator pedal, the shift indicator lamp signals that you can get the same performance with less fuel by shifting up without losing power.

Tests conducted by Saab and the EPA compared operation of cars that had an upshift indicator to those that did not. In the EPA city-driving test, use of the indicator yielded an average gas mileage improvement of more than 9 percent. Even without such an indicator, you should shift into a higher gear sooner than you normally would and use fifth gear as much as possible to stretch your fuel.

Watch the tachometer

Because tachometers are no longer limited to performance models, more drivers than ever have a chance to pay attention to engine speed as well as road speed. This allows you to find the engine's most efficient rpm and stay close to that point whenever feasible. What speed is that?

The exact figure depends on the engine but is typically the speed at which it produces the greatest torque output. For economy's sake, it's generally wise to remain below 3,000 rpm most of the time and to shift into the next gear before the engine gets much beyond its optimum rpm level. Too low an engine speed does nothing for your finances, so running below 1,500 isn't ordinarily a good idea.

Skip an occasional gear

No rule says you have to use each gear of your manual transmission every time, going through a never-changing

1-2-3-4-5 sequence. Try going directly from first to third (skipping second); or go from second to fourth without using third. This technique is especially useful if heavy traffic has caused you to rev too high in the lower gear already, as when merging onto an expressway from the entry lane.

Get the most from your automatic transmission

An automatic transmission liberates you from shifting gears yourself, but nothing is free, and an engine must work a little harder and use a bit more gas to transmit power through an automatic transmission than a manual. For proof, look no further than EPA fuel economy estimates, which are invariably lower for an automatic transmission than for that same vehicle equipped with a manual transmission.

Still, there are some things you can do to maximize fuel efficiency in an automatic-transmission vehicle.

During acceleration, listen as the engine note rises and then falls to get a sense of when the transmission is reaching the "top" of one gear ratio and changing down to the next lower ratio. Also, watch the needle on the tachometer climb up the rpm range and descend correspondingly. Remember, the higher the rpm, the more fuel you're burning.

Some automatic transmissions tend to stay in lower gears a little too long for peak economy. You can sometimes coax the transmission into shifting to high gear earlier than usual by letting up on the gas as you pass 30 mph or so. Then, once it's in top gear, continue to accelerate very gradually.

That little OD light

Virtually all manual and automatic transmissions have an overdrive gear that can be employed to save fuel. It's usually the highest-numbered gear (or gears), and it lets the engine run at a slower speed (or lower rpm) while the car maintains the same road speed.

If you're looking to save gas, get into an overdrive gear as soon as possible and stay there until you need the extra power afforded by a lower gear.

With an automatic transmission, a lot of that decision making is out of your hands. Automatics tend to move to the highest gear on their own, precisely to save fuel; at cruising speeds, overdrive (OD) kicks in. But you can shift into and out of OD. On newer cars, it's usually done via a button on the shift lever. Typically, an "OD" light illuminates in the instrument panel when an automatic is shifted out of OD. If you have inadvertently shifted out of OD, press the button to get back in for optimal fuel economy.

Drive 55

Not only are highway speed limits the law, but they're also set to help you save money. It's a simple law of physics: The higher the speed, the greater the air resistance a car has to buck. The EPA estimates a mileage boost of about 15 percent by driving at 55 mph rather than 65. Every automobile has an optimum speed at which it delivers the best gas mileage—and that speed is rarely above 50 mph.

Many modern automatic transmissions allow drivers to change gears manually by moving the shift lever through a separate gate. This doesn't duplicate the degree of gear control afforded by a manual transmission, but it will allow you to select a lower gear for more throttle response. Doing so increases engine rpm and burns more gas. For best fuel efficiency, shift into the highest gear whenever possible or simply shift into Drive and let the automatic do what it's designed to: Select the most economical gear at each step of the way.

Make sure nothing's afoot

Don't drive with a foot resting on the brake pedal, however lightly. Even the slightest application of the brakes while moving will drag down fuel economy. It'll place an unnecessary burden on the engine and transmission. You'll wear out your brakes rapidly, as well.

SAVING GAS WHILE SITTING STILL

Shift to neutral when stopped

If you're not moving but your engine is running, you're getting zero miles per gallon. Idling at a traffic light is a fuel-economy killer, as is waiting to clear a construction zone or sitting while a freight train crawls by. And there's a good reason our most frustrating traffic condition is called stop-and-go driving.

Notice that shifting your automatic or manual transmission into neutral calms down your engine note and drops the rpm. That saves gas. Shift into neutral even for a long traffic light.

Keeping an automatic transmission in Drive puts an extra load on it, which drains fuel. In neutral, it's resting— or at least as close to rest as an automatic ever gets. This shift is even more important when the air conditioner is running, so the engine doesn't have to strain so hard while idling. A manual transmission should be shifted to neutral at every stop.

Shut off the engine when stopped

Even when stopped for a mile-long freight train, a lot of drivers keep their engines running. A minute of idling, however, consumes more gas than a restart.

So, whenever you expect to be stopped for a minute or more, shut off the ignition. No, not at every red light you come to, though some experts advise that even a 30-second stop is worth a shutdown. Use your judgment, but when standing in a bank drive-up line or at a fast-food drive-through, if it looks like a long wait without moving, turn off that engine.

Note that the new gas/electric hybrid vehicles automatically shut off the gas engine in most conditions if the vehicle is stopped for even a few seconds. They restart instantly as the gas pedal is applied. The engineers who designed those hybrids know the fuel-saving value of shutting off an engine.

Don't race the engine at stoplights

It's hard to understand why people are inclined to tromp on the pedal—sometimes every couple of seconds—while waiting for a green light. What's to be gained, except drawing attention to yourself?

If you need to pump the pedal to keep the engine from dying, chances are fuel economy isn't your major worry—in fact, you need to consult a mechanic!

On an upgrade, hang on with the brake

When waiting at a stoplight or stop sign on an upward pavement, keep the car from drifting backward by pressing on the brake pedal in the normal manner. Don't use the clutch or automatic transmission to keep it from sliding back. This wastes fuel and puts a strain on the engine.

Shut down when you leave the car

If it's a good idea to shut off the engine even when stopped for a minute while you're still in the driver's seat, obviously it's essential to do so when you stop and leave your car for awhile. Don't leave the engine idle while making a phone call, hopping into a store, or dropping off the dry cleaning. Sure, that might keep the interior warm in winter or cool in summer, but the gasoline is just burning away, accomplishing no useful purpose—to say nothing of the fact that an idling car is just begging for a thief to drive it off.

Park it now

If you're a city dweller, you know that finding that perfect parking spot is nearly impossible. Why even try? Don't waste time and fuel cruising for an ideal spot that is steps away from your destination. Pick the one that comes along first, even if it means walking a few blocks. The exercise will do you good.

In the same vein, park so you don't have to move your vehicle a short time later. Don't leave it sitting on the street or in the driveway so that you have to move it into the garage. By that time, the engine has cooled down, and you're wasting gas to start the car while putting extra wear on its parts.

Don't rev the engine before shutting off the ignition

Many of us learned to do this on carburetor-equipped engines in the belief that stomping the gas pedal as we turned off the switch would "prime" the carb (put a jolt of gasoline in its bowl). Most of the time, it did little or no good even for a carbureted engine.

For today's fuel-injected engines, it's a complete waste of fuel. Not only that, but the final spurt of gasoline also winds up dumped on the cylinder walls where it can wash away the essential lubricant, paving the way for increased wear.

ACCESSORIES AND OTHER TRICKS

Don't flip that switch!

Nearly every option and accessory on a car carries a penalty in gas mileage. Why? To start with, each adds weight: maybe a little, maybe a lot, but every pound that has to be hauled demands more fuel to do the job. Second, most of those convenient extras operate from electricity, and electricity comes at a price: fuel consumption.

Take care with air

The impact on the fuel economy of accessories, such as heated seats or a high-powered audio system, is measured in tenths of a mile per gallon. The air conditioner can knock mileage down by whole units.

The compressor that runs your vehicle's air conditioner demands a huge amount of energy, which puts a massive drain on the engine. Use of the air conditioner, however, doesn't always result in a dramatic drop in fuel mileage. Sometimes, using the air conditioner saves fuel.

Running the A/C in stop-and-go traffic can cost you up to 4 mpg because the engine simply isn't being revved enough to offset the load placed on it by the compressor. On the highway, however, as the engine is already turning at a low-stress rpm, the fuel costs associated with A/C are far less extreme.

As you approach the speed limit, it can actually be cheaper to run the air conditioner than to open the windows. Why? Because open windows create severe aerodynamic drag as the vehicle's body tries to glide through the air.

The trade-off between open windows and running the A/C tips at about 50 mph. Below that, you're more economical with the windows open. Above that, running the A/C will actually save you fuel.

To save fuel any time you run the A/C, set the temperature control somewhere above frigid cold. That keeps the compressor from running constantly. Use your climate system's economy setting or a warmer level on the temperature selector.

Close the windows—open the vents

Instead of making a choice between air-conditioning and open windows on the road, you could simply rely on the car's ventilation system. Just open one or two windows slightly, in addition to opening the vents. Except on really stifling days or when moving slowly through traffic, it might keep the car nearly as cool as with "air."

Unfortunately, not every modern car's vents deliver a suitably cool breeze. Study your owner's manual to see how your system works best. For such a simple notion, some systems are surprisingly complex, with a bewildering selection of fresh-airflow possibilities. Opening the rear windows or a minivan's rear vents helps airflow.

Headlights and fuel economy

It is important to make yourself visible while driving, and that means liberal use of headlights. It is advisable to switch on your headlights at the hint of dusk or in even slightly overcast conditions. And use them on twisty country roads no matter what the light conditions are.

Some vehicles, notably those from General Motors, take care of that for you with daytime running lights (DRLs). These illuminate the headlamps anytime the ignition is switched on. Safety studies show DRLs make vehicles more visible to other drivers, and nearly all published reports indicate DRLs reduce multiple-vehicle daytime crashes.

Of course, headlights use electrical power, and generating that power burns some fuel. But the National Highway Traffic Safety Administration estimates DRLs cost just a fraction of a mile per gallon, depending on the type of system used. Most DRLs operate headlamps at less than

normal power during daylight hours, thereby conserving
energy and reducing the effect on a vehicle's fuel economy.

Granted, using headlights during the day can shorten
bulb life. But whether you switch them on yourself or drive
a vehicle equipped with DRLs, it's only a few extra dollars
per year in fuel costs and bulb-replacement expenses.
That's a small price to pay for added safety.

Use cruise control prudently

This often-misunderstood device can save gas when operated properly at the correct time. "Cruise" is just the ticket
for driving those long, flat stretches. Not only can you
relax your right foot and not worry about the speedometer
reading, but cruise control can often maintain speed better
than you can manage manually. And what does steady
speed bring? That's right: better gas mileage.

LIVE EFFICIENTLY

What is "energy"? Where does it come from? And how do we pay for it? When you learn the answers to these questions, you can also learn how to live more efficiently in your home.

- **Be smart about how you use energy.**

- **Know when to turn your electrical power on and off.**

- **Use natural gas, propane, and fuel oil in the most effective way.**

THE BIG PICTURE

Basic concepts of energy efficiency in a home

You can make a lot of progress toward improving the energy efficiency in your home by simply plugging the many places through which air can get in or get out. Plugging your home is called "air sealing," and it is one of the most important first steps to take when weatherizing your house to increase its energy efficiency. Many of the tips in this book's later chapters pertain to finding and sealing up holes in your home.

Increasing the amount of insulation in various places in your home should be a high priority. Insulation, in its many forms, helps stop the transfer of heat from one place to another. A good example of this is the insulation in your attic. A thick layer of insulation helps stop heat flow from the house to the attic during the winter. In the summer, that same insulation helps stop heat transfer from the hot attic to the rooms below.

But while better air sealing and insulation in your home can do a lot to reduce your utility bill, that's not where the story on energy efficiency starts and ends. There are many other ways to conserve, some of which require only simple changes of habit or lifestyle.

Electricity powers lights, appliances, and electronic devices in your home. It also runs air conditioners, heats water, cooks food, dries laundry, and in some cases is used for space heating. Natural gas, propane, and oil are mostly burned to provide space heating and hot water; and secondary uses for these gases include cooking, clothes drying, and fireplace fuel.

Electricity

Electricity enters a home through a service-entry cable either above or below ground. From there it passes through a main electrical service panel containing fuses or breakers and is distributed throughout the house through wires, receptacles, and switches. Electricity is billed to the consumer by the kilowatt-hour (kWH). Each kWH costs approximately 8 to 15 cents, depending on where you live and your utility company's fees.

One kilowatt-hour equals 1,000 watts of electricity used for an hour. To understand how kilowatts are calculated, picture a 100-watt lightbulb. Burning that bulb for one hour uses 100 watts of electricity. If it burns for 10 hours, that equals one kilowatt (100 watts × 10 hours = 1,000 watts, or one kilowatt). And burning that one bulb for those 10 hours costs between 8 and 15 cents.

Natural gas

Natural gas is delivered to homes through a network of underground pipes. After natural gas passes through a meter outside of a house, the gas is piped to where it is needed inside—to a furnace or boiler, water heater, or gas fireplace—through a series of smaller metal pipes. Natural gas is billed to the consumer by the cubic foot of gas used.

Propane

Propane, or liquefied petroleum gas (LPG), is transported by truck from a utility or gas company to a storage tank on a homeowner's property outside the home. From there it enters the house through a pipe and is distributed via a system similar to that used for natural gas. Propane is billed by the gallon.

Oil

Fuel oil is also transported by truck, is pumped into a storage tank either inside or outside the house, and is piped to the appliances where it is needed. Fuel oil is billed by the gallon as well.

So that's how energy arrives at your house and how it is billed. What happens after that—how you use these energy supplies—has everything to do with how large your utility bill is at the end of the month. Every time you turn on a light or a TV, use hot water, or switch on the air conditioner or furnace, you consume energy.

ENERGY-EFFICIENT LIVING

Dial down and save

In 1977, President Jimmy Carter appeared on national television for the first of what were later dubbed "energy speeches." The country was going through an oil crisis, and Carter advised us to "dial down" our thermostats. His line of reasoning was that, by reducing the temperature in our homes, we could conserve heating fuel.

President Carter's words of nearly 30 years ago still ring true today: The best way to conserve energy is to not use so much of it. And one of the best ways of reducing the use of heating fuel in the home is to simply turn down the thermostat.

Because space heating constitutes the largest energy expenditure in many homes, even a little conservation of heating fuel goes a long way toward achieving a lower utility bill. Dialing down the thermostat one degree during the winter can result in about 1 to 3 percent less fuel use, and a similar reduction in your heating bill.

Dialing down details—and a fashion statement

A furnace or boiler has to maintain a differential in temperature between the inside of the house and the outdoors in order for the house to feel comfortable. On cold days that difference can be as much as 50–60 degrees (say, 20 out-

side and 70 inside). Any time the differential can be reduced, even by a degree or two, the heating system comes
on less often, less fuel is burned, and savings result. The
downside of turning down a thermostat, of course, is that
the house is cooler. But Carter had a solution for that—
simply slip on a sweater. That makes sense, too. Instead of
turning up the heat to increase the overall warmth in the
huge volume of space inside the house, you can simply
increase your personal insulation to help retain body heat.

Though dialing down might seem a hardship at first,
after a while your body will adjust to the "new normal"
house temperature and wearing sweaters and socks inside
will become a part of everyday life. (More information
on dialing down your thermostat at night and during the
hours when you're away from the house—and on digital
thermostats that can be used to automate and simplify the
process—can be found in the following chapter, "Increase
Energy Efficiency.")

Dialing up and dressing appropriately for the heat

The concept of dialing down can be reversed for energy
savings during the warm months. "Dialing up" is an effective method of reducing the cost of cooling a house with
room or central air-conditioning.

The same principles apply: The less the temperature
differential the air-conditioning system has to maintain
between the inside and outside, the less often the compressor comes on, the less electricity is consumed, and the
lower the utility bill.

Instead of setting the thermostat to the point that the
air-conditioning system makes the house cold, try dialing it

up a few degrees and adjusting your clothing to deal with the slightly warmer temperature. Chances are you'll never notice the difference. And, as is the case with heating, dialing the thermostat up when you're away from the house results in lower energy consumption.

Heat less space

If there are rooms in your house that aren't being used, shutting the doors to those rooms results in an overall reduction in the amount of area that the heating and air-conditioning systems have to heat and cool. When a child moves away from home to go to college, or when parts of the basement aren't being used, isolating those areas from the rest of the house means less demand in terms of heating and cooling, and a lower energy bill. The less space you need to supply with conditioned air, the less often the heating, ventilation, and air-conditioning (HVAC) systems will need to operate.

Under the covers

Many people prefer to "sleep cold," and they don't mind turning down the thermostat into the low 60s or mid 50s at night. Some even like to turn off the heat entirely in the bedroom and sleep with a window open. Those who are comfortable dialing back this dramatically are able to reduce their heating fuel consumption substantially at night, as the heating system does not have to maintain a large temperature differential between the inside and outside.

For those not so inclined, there are means available to stay warm under the covers, even while dialing back the thermostat. Down or synthetic-filled comforters provide insulation with little weight. And electric blankets generate warmth at a small cost in electrical energy.

HOME ENERGY MANAGEMENT AND CONTROL

Winter cold

If you're willing to be active in managing your home's energy resources, there are many opportunities not only to conserve heat and air-conditioning but also to reduce the burden on your heat and air-conditioning systems.

Though it's 93 million miles away from Earth, our sun puts out some pretty potent energy. It is smart house management to take advantage of that free heat whenever possible. In the winter, opening up shades and drapes on south-facing windows allows sunlight inside the house where it can warm floors, furniture, and furnishings. This is called passive solar heating, and on a sunny day in a well-insulated house it can reduce the number of times your heating system has to activate. One bonus is that during the winter the sun is lower on the horizon, so sunlight penetrates deeper into the house than it does when almost directly overhead in the summer. Therefore, even though the winter sun's rays are less intense, they can still create heat because they cover more surface area in your house.

At night in winter, heavy or insulating shades and drapes drawn over the windows will keep heat inside, acting as both a radiant heat barrier for heat leaving the home and also as insulation over the cold window glazing.

Taking advantage of the sun during the winter can also help lower electricity bills. Though sunlight streaming in through windows is only a heating benefit on the east, south, and west sides of the house, opening shades on the north side of the house in the daytime reduces the need for electrical lighting.

Summer heat
During the summer you'll want to do the direct opposite—close shades and drapes in order to keep the warming rays of sunlight out of the house, reducing the load on the cooling system.

Fan out
The use of central or room air-conditioning (and the high electrical costs associated with each) can be reduced by deploying a time-honored strategy—getting the air around you to move. A simple desktop or standing fan that sweeps the room every few seconds makes the air seem cooler by several degrees.

Ceiling fans are a great boon in this regard since they gently move all of the air in a room at once. Ceiling fans can draw up and distribute the cooler air that lies along the floor throughout the entire room.

Lights out
Though it's a simple energy-saving step, the concept of turning off lights when leaving a room seems to elude many people who subsequently complain about their utility bills. The fact is, if a light is off, it uses no electricity. So only turn on lights that are necessary for use. It's that easy to save energy.

Do Ceiling Fans Cool a Room When It Is Unoccupied?

No, ceiling fans do not create cool air. The air passing over your skin has a "wind chill" effect that makes you feel cooler. But the air itself does not decrease in temperature.

In fact, since a ceiling fan is powered by an electrical motor, as the motor turns, it actually creates a little bit of heat.

Using ceiling fans is a good way to limit the amount of time an air-conditioning system has to run in the summer. But it's best to use them only when there are people in the room to enjoy the effects of the passing air and to turn them off when the occupants depart. Leaving them on all the time does not cool the air in the house and wastes electricity.

Those without ceiling fans but with a forced-air furnace have the option of switching on the furnace's blower fan to help move warm and stagnant air. On most thermostats there is a fan setting between "off" and "auto." That setting is "on," and it simply switches the fan on to run continuously. Running the furnace blower fan for a few hours every day—at far less cost than it takes to operate a room or central air-conditioning system—can reduce the need for the more energy-consumptive cooling.

One urban myth says that turning on a light uses far more energy than it consumes while it is operating. Not so. It is true that when an incandescent or fluorescent light-

bulb is first switched on, it requires a brief surge of electricity. But that surge is so short that it doesn't make any
practical difference. With fluorescents, the electricity consumed during start-up is equivalent to only a few seconds'
worth of running the light. So keep bulbs that aren't being
used turned off.

ENERGY-EFFICIENT KITCHEN PRACTICES

What's cooking?

In the winter, firing up a gas or electric oven or range contributes to the heat needed to keep the house warm. So,
in addition to the smells of cooking food, you also receive
the benefit of the extra heat from the oven and range top's
burners or heating elements.

That heat is unwelcome in the summer. And if the home
has air-conditioning, those systems are called upon to
remove the heat and dump it outside the house. Therefore,
during summertime, conventional cooking practices are
doubly inefficient. First you generate heat you don't need
or want, and then the A/C has to come on to remove it from
the house.

For optimum energy efficiency, it makes sense in any
season to use cooking appliances appropriate to the volume and type of food being cooked. Baking a few potatoes
can be accomplished quickly and at much less energy cost
in a microwave oven than they would require using a conventional oven. Countertop toaster ovens and broilers can

prepare a wide variety of foods, and they don't produce the amount of heat or consume nearly the energy that a full-size range does.

When possible, cook foods together in the oven that require similar temperatures. And use lids on pots on the range top not only to prevent heat from escaping the top of the pot but also to reduce cooking time. An oven or range-top burner can often be shut off before the food is completely cooked, and the food can be allowed to "coast" until it's ready, using the heat built up inside the pot or pan. If this prevents the oven's burner from firing up one last time, that's energy saved.

A lot of hot air

Ventilation is important in a kitchen to remove cooking odors, humidity, heat, and combustion by-products from gas ranges and ovens. Most kitchens are outfitted with a hood or microwave over the range that comes with filters to strain grease and other pollutants out of the air. Some range hoods, however, do not vent directly to the outside of the house. So although they may filter some cooking grease and oil out of the air, they are ineffective in terms of removing heat, humidity, and combustion pollutants from the kitchen environment. An upgrade to a true outside-venting range hood can help remove cooking heat from the house, reducing the need for air-conditioning in the summer.

Big batches

In busy families it makes sense from a logistical and time-management point of view to make large batches of frequently eaten foods, like soups and spaghetti sauce, to be frozen for later use. Volume food processing like this also pays energy dividends. It takes much less energy to turn on the range once to cook a big pot of something rather than to turn it on multiple times to cook smaller portions.

In from the cold; refrigerator issues

Refrigerators consume a relatively large portion of the household energy budget, but there are several simple things you can do to get the most bang for your refrigeration buck.

Just as combining driving trips in your car reduces the amount of gasoline your car guzzles, it makes sense to open the refrigerator door once to remove all the food you need at any one time. Opening the door repeatedly pulls cool air from within and causes the compressor to come on, making your electric meter spin. Anticipate what you're going to remove from the refrigerator, open it, remove what you need, and then quickly close it again.

It's also a good idea to allow warm foods to cool to room temperature before moving them to the refrigerator. That way energy won't be required to do work that can take place naturally. In the winter, leaving warm foods to cool outside of the refrigerator (if this can be safely accomplished from a food-safety standpoint) contributes a small amount of heat to the house.

Condensation control switch

Many people don't realize it, but most newer refrigerators incorporate small heating elements in their fronts. Why does a refrigerator need a heater? To prevent condensation in the area where the doors contact the front of the cabinet.

The narrow space between the upper freezer and lower refrigerator on conventional top-freezer refrigerators, and along the sides of those areas, are difficult to insulate adequately. As the compressor and refrigerant cool the interior of the fridge, some of the cold leaks out onto the steel cabinet enclosure. On a humid day, moisture in the air condenses on those cool surfaces just as it would on a cold beverage glass in the summer. When this happens repeatedly, mildew and mold can begin to form on the surface of the refrigerator in these areas, as well as on the vinyl door gaskets.

The solution to this problem is to insert tiny heating elements in the front of the refrigerator, just large enough to slightly warm those front surfaces to the point that condensation no longer forms. While the heaters don't draw a large amount of electricity, they're on constantly. That's fine in the summer when the feature is needed. But in the winter the heaters are not required in the generally drier indoor air, so that electricity is going to waste.

Refrigerators equipped with these condensation-prevention heaters contain a small control box, usually on the back wall. Alongside a switch in the control box might be a label that says "Prevents Condensation/Saves Energy—On/Off." During the winter, simply moving that switch from the On to the Off position will shut down the heaters, thus saving electricity.

Dishpan hands

Washing dishes by hand is never high on anyone's list of favorite activities. Techniques for doing this mundane task, however, can save energy. Domestic water heating makes up nearly a quarter of the typical family's utility bill, but intelligent use of hot water while dishwashing can reduce that by a significant amount.

A surprising number of people attack the task of dishwashing by first opening the hot water faucet to its "full Niagara" position and then running dirty dishes in and out of the stream to first wash and then rinse. In the process of cleaning up after a meal they waste gallons of water—and also the energy that heated that water.

A better way to wash dishes by hand is to close up the drain and run a couple of inches of hot water in the bottom of a sink, along with some liquid dish detergent. Then turn off the faucet. Wash glasses, cups, and silverware in this soap-concentrated water, and rinse off the soap over the same sink filled with water. The hot water used for rinsing runs into the sink, filling it up further for the larger items to come. And the soap used to wash these first items is retained as well.

Next stack plates in the soapy water and start washing them. Remove them as each is washed, and stack them in the bottom of the adjacent sink. When a good pile has accumulated, run water over the stack and remove and rinse each plate in turn. The water running from the plates as they are removed helps do a preliminary rinse on the next plate below, allowing it to do "double duty" on its way down the drain.

When everything has been washed, don't drain the wash water out of the sink yet. There are several gallons of hot water left in there—water you paid to heat. Allowing it to cool off gradually adds some heat to the kitchen, which forestalls the furnace or boiler from coming on. In the summer you'll want to drain the hot water as quickly as possible in order to avoid adding its heat to the air-conditioning load.

Automatic dishwashers

Newer dishwashers on the market are more energy efficient than earlier models, and they use less water for each load. But there are still some tricks for using them that can further decrease their water and energy usage.

Newer dishwashers are equipped with sensors that determine how long the wash cycle runs in order to get dishes clean. The sensors detect food particles in the wash water. As long as the sensors "see" food particles in the wash water, the wash cycle will continue. Knowing that, the inclination is to rinse each dish nearly clean before putting it into the dishwasher. Bad idea.

Rinsing dishes under running water wastes water that you paid to heat. The dishwasher is going to use water to go through a cycle anyway, so let it do its job and clean the dishes the way it was designed. Rinsing the dishes before putting them into the dishwasher essentially consumes enough water to wash them twice. In addition, rinsing the dishes actually fools the internal sensors into believing that the wash cycle is nearly complete before it has had time to work. With few food particles to sense, the cycle goes almost immediately to rinse. The result can be dirty dishes once you open the door.

Modern dishwashers give you the option of using heat and a fan to dry the dishes. That heat is provided by an electrical coil in the bottom of the unit. Resistance heating coils like this require electricity, so shutting that feature off if you don't require instant drying will result in electrical energy savings.

ENERGY-EFFICIENT LAUNDRY AND BATHING

Here are some methods to reduce energy consumption in the laundry room and the bathroom by decreasing hot water usage and minimizing the operation of appliances.

Detergent operas

Though it might be difficult to make the connection at first, in recent years lowly laundry detergent has become an impact player in the field of energy conservation. Cold-water detergents clean nearly every type of clothing as well as conventional detergents, and because water does not need to be heated in order to make them work, energy savings can be realized on laundry day. Because most clothes can be washed in cold water (and doing so also helps prevent dye color from bleeding), it's a good idea to take advantage of this advance in detergent technology.

In areas where the water entering the home during the winter is quite cold, liquid detergent works better than a powder, as most powders do not dissolve as well in cold water as they do in warm.

Fill 'er up

It is important too, for both water and energy savings, to do full loads of laundry whenever possible. Running a washing machine to do one large load as opposed to several smaller ones uses less electricity to power the machine's motor, and overall water consumption will be lower as well. So letting laundry stack up a bit is not a sign of laziness; it's saving energy.

Hang 'em high

Clothes dryers tumble clothing inside a heated drum to remove moisture soaked up during the washing process. The heat is produced by electricity, or natural or propane gas. But you can avoid using any energy at all (well, except some of your own) to dry clothes by using the sun and wind to do the job. Clotheslines and folding dryers are inexpensive, and it takes only a few minutes to hang a load of wash. The sun sanitizes the clothing, and everything smells fresh.

An alternative to hanging clothing outside in the winter is to set up a place inside for drying, usually in the basement. If your house is dry during the winter, the evaporating water from the drying clothes adds welcome moisture to the air. In homes that already have adequate humidity, however, excess moisture can bring on problems like condensation on walls and ceilings, and subsequent mildew and mold growth.

Another point in favor of hanging clothing to dry has to do with how using a dryer ages and deteriorates clothing. High heat breaks down material fibers and causes them to fracture and loosen—that is, after all, what dryer lint consists of; broken-off fibers. The tumbling action of clothing rubbing against other clothing is also abrasive, further deteriorating the material. So, outside line drying pays off not only in terms of energy efficiency but also in clothing longevity.

Hot teeth?

Saving energy in a household can involve some simple habit changing. Here's an example. Say you're a person who always washes your face before brushing your teeth. Your bathroom is on the upper floor of a two-story house, and it takes a while for the hot water to make its way up the two floors and finally into the faucet at the sink. To save a bit of energy and water, try brushing your teeth first before you wash your face. You're going to use cold water to brush your teeth anyway, so why not use that first portion of cold water at the hot water tap to do the job?

Then, because you've opened the hot water tap and started the hot water up the pipe, your wait for the hot water will be shorter, and you'll waste less water while waiting. This is a simple trick that, admittedly, does not amount to very much on its own. But multiply it by 365 days a year, and you'll save quite a bit of hot water.

Shorter showers, smaller baths

One of the mantras of energy conservation is doing more with less. This also means not using so much in the first place. In the U.S. Navy, sailors take what is referred to as a "Navy shower" in order to conserve fresh water on-board ship. You stand in the shower, get yourself wet, shut off the shower, soap up, and then turn the shower back on to rinse off. Some modern showerheads come with a simple shut-off valve located near the nozzle that allows you to turn off the flow of water and turn it back on again without affecting the temperature setting. Doing this a few times makes you realize how wasteful a 20-minute shower really is; you can get just as clean and use a lot less water in the shower.

Ditto in regard to the bath. Filling a bathtub an inch or two lower is unlikely to make any difference from a hygiene standpoint, and the water and energy saved add up.

Also, consider taking a shower instead of a bath in the first place. A shower, if it's kept to a reasonable length, usually requires less water than a bath.

Leave the water in the tub

When you're finished in the bath, consider leaving the water in the tub for a few hours. Similar to the case with a sink full of dishwashing water, you paid to heat that water, and allowing it to cool off inside the house adds some heat to the bathroom. Additionally, in a dry house during the winter, the bathwater will add some needed humidity to the air. Of course, you'll want to do the opposite during the summer; the sooner you can get the bathwater to run out of the tub the better. That way it won't add its heat to the air where the air-conditioning will have to remove it.

Buy early and save!

The price of propane gas and fuel oil fluctuates over the course of the year. If you use either of these heating fuels, purchasing them in the summer often means you'll pay less per gallon than you would if you waited until fall to fill up the tank. Though it can be difficult to contemplate locking up several hundred dollars in fuel that you won't use for months, doing so can result in some big savings that you'll appreciate when the cold weather begins.

INCREASE ENERGY EFFICIENCY

There are plenty of no-cost or low-cost alterations you can make to your home to increase its energy efficiency.

- **Set your water heater at 130 degrees for best results.**

- **Dial your thermostat up or down to cut your energy bills.**

- **Turn off unneeded standing pilot lights and use compact fluorescent light.**

WINDOWS AND WATER HEATER

Lock 'em up

Here's a no-cost, minimal-labor tip that reduces air infiltration into and out of your house during both summer and winter. It also helps provide better security for your family. Lock your windows!

That's right. Just a simple trip around the inside of your house to be sure all the window locks are engaged can save energy. The reason? Most windows, both casement and double-hung types, are made with compressible weather stripping that helps seal out air infiltration along the edges and between the upper and lower sash. The locks on casement windows draw the sash closer to the frame (in the case of double-hung windows, they're closer together in the middle), and that compresses the weather stripping, creating a more airtight seal.

Windows are designed to provide light and ventilation. They should also seal well in order to prevent air and water leakage. If your windows aren't locked when they're not open, you're not using one of the features that contribute to their energy performance.

Water heater temperature settings

The cost of heating water for your home may amount to as much as 15–20 percent of your entire utility bill. Setting your water heater's temperature in the 130-degree range instead of a higher one requires less energy to heat and to hold the water. Every 10 degrees you dial down the thermostat can knock 3–5 percent off your water-heating bill. In addition, a lower hot water temperature reduces the chance of scalding.

By setting your water heater to 130 degrees, you should produce 120-degree water at the tap, which is low enough to prevent injury but still hot enough to produce a satisfyingly warm shower or bath. There is always some heat loss in the piping between the water heater and the fixtures where the water is used, so that's why the water heater's temperature should be in the 130-degree range, which is also sufficiently hot to prevent bacteria from growing inside the water heater's tank.

Degree Days

Heating and cooling contractors use "degree days" as a mathematical tool to help determine how much energy you could save by upgrading to higher efficiency HVAC equipment. There are two types of degree days: heating degree days and cooling degree days.

Heating degree days are calculated by adding the warmest and the coldest temperature recorded in an area during a 24-hour period. That sum is divided by two and then subtracted from 65 degrees. Each degree of temperature below 65 is called one degree day. An example:

Highest temperature	40 degrees
Lowest temperature	22 degrees
Total	**62 degrees**

divided by 2
= 31 degrees

65 degrees minus 31 degrees = **34 degrees**

So, on this particular day, there were 34 heating "degree days."

Cooling degree days are calculated the same way, except that once you've determined your average temperature, you subtract 65 from that number, instead of vice versa. Thus, any degrees of temperature above

Gas and oil water heaters can be adjusted easily by turning the dial thermostat on the front of the control box. There may be degree markings on the dial, but many have

65 degrees in the final sum are counted as cooling degree days. An example:

Highest temperature	90 degrees
Lowest temperature	74 degrees
Total	**164 degrees**

$$\text{divided by } 2$$
$$= 82 \text{ degrees}$$

82 degrees minus 65 degrees = **17 degrees**

So, on this particular day, there were 17 cooling degree days.

Duluth, Minnesota, with 9,756 heating degree days, has one of the highest totals in the lower 48 states, while Orlando, Florida, has one of the lowest with 733. The National Weather Service's Web site at http://www.cpc.ncep.noaa.gov/products/analysis_monitoring/cdus/degree_days/DDF_index.shtml predicts heating and cooling degree days for the entire country.

Homeowners who live in areas with a high number of heating degree days receive a faster payback on an investment in energy efficient heating equipment than those who live in areas with lower numbers of heating degree days. Conversely, homeowners who live in areas with a high number of cooling degree days benefit from faster payback on energy-efficient cooling equipment than those who live in colder climes.

simple arrows that point the direction to "hot" and "not-so-hot" settings. You might have to experiment by gradually turning down the dial over the course of several days in order to arrive at a setting that feels comfortable to you and your family.

Adjusting the temperature setting on an electric water heater is slightly more complicated and may require removing coverings over the heating elements. Small screws attached to the elements can usually be turned to the temperature of your choice. Most have painted or engraved temperature reading marks on the screw housing. Both heating elements must be dialed to the same degree reading or one might never activate. Check your owner's manual before you adjust an electric water heater to ensure you're following the proper procedure for your particular model. Be sure to shut off the power before you remove any protective cover plates.

It may require a day or so for the water in any type of heater to stabilize to the new temperature setting after an adjustment has been made to the thermostatic control. Test the water temperature by running a tap until the water is hot, then fill a glass with the water. Put a thermometer in the glass, and take a reading.

There are other good reasons to dial down your water heater's thermostat. Higher water heater temperatures can contribute to early failure of the tank. Because chemical reactions are speeded up in hotter environments, rusting of the steel tank is accelerated under high temperature conditions. Plus, sediment (hard-water minerals) precipitates out of hard water more rapidly in hotter conditions. It collects at the tank's bottom and reduces the energy efficiency of the water heater. For energy savings, safety, and equipment longevity, dialing back your water heater thermostat to 130 degrees or so (about 120 at the tap) makes sense.

THERMOSTAT

Nighttime is the right time to dial down

While the concept of dialing down your house temperature a few degrees during your home's occupied hours is helpful in terms of energy conservation, it's at night and when you're away from the house that you can turn down the thermostat even more, thus significantly reducing your energy bill.

The question often arises, "How long does the thermostat have to be at a low setting in order to save enough energy to make up for what it takes to get the house back up to temperature when you dial the heat back up?"

Experts at the Department of Energy have determined that the amount of energy saved as the temperature falls in a house after the thermostat is dialed down is approximately equal to that used to get the house up to temperature again. The actual energy savings in a dialed-down session occur during the time when the heat is operating at its lowest setting. At that point the heating system does not have to work as hard to maintain a large indoor temperature differential compared to the outdoors.

In other words, the amount of energy saved by turning down the thermostat makes up for the energy used in turning it back up. Meanwhile, any hours spent with a smaller temperature difference between indoors and outdoors results in the system not having to come on as often; that's where the savings lie. And the lower you dial, the more savings you can realize.

HVAC experts estimate that for every degree the thermostat is dialed down, you can save 1–3 percent on your heating or cooling utility bill. And when you count up the many hours you're either in bed or the home is not occupied, there is considerable potential for savings.

Digital thermostat features

In recent years the marketplace has seen an influx of sophisticated, programmable digital thermostats that assist periodic dialing down, or temperature "setback." For an investment of $40 to $100, these thermostats can be programmed to automatically dial down the heat at a certain time at night or when you're away from the house and to turn it up again before you awake in the morning or arrive home. The automated features of a digital thermostat ensure that you will never have to dial back the heat at night manually, and you can wake up to a house that is up to its normal temperature in the morning.

Digital thermostats are also more accurate than the older-style mercury switch units; they can differentiate room temperature down to a fraction of a degree. This precision results in more exact control of the HVAC system, eliminating large temperature swings, and thus delivers better comfort—as well as energy savings—from the setback function. The programming features can also help in the summer when setting the thermostat to allow the temperature to rise in the house while you're away (in order to avoid having the A/C come on as often) saves energy.

Basic digital thermostats might allow you to program time and setback temperatures using two schedules—one for the five-day work week and another for the weekend. Higher-end models pack more options and sophisticated features, such as the ability to program different setback and wake-up settings separately for every day of the week. This can be helpful if you need to rise at different times on different days. And all digital thermostats can be over-ridden at any time to accommodate a specific need, such as a house full of people you'd like to keep cool during a summer party.

If you're thinking of investing in a digital thermostat, be aware that there are several types to fit different configurations of HVAC systems. The thermostat must fit the system in order to work properly. You'll have to know how many wires run to your old thermostat in order to match it with the new digital model.

As a side note, if an old thermostat you're replacing has a mercury switch (look for a small glass vial inside that holds a silvery liquid), it must be handled carefully to avoid breakage and be disposed of properly. Mercury is a toxin and an environmental hazard! If the manufacturer of the thermostat you purchase doesn't directly engage in a recycling program, take it to your nearest hazardous material recycling center.

Let your fingers do the walking

If you're not technologically inclined, or if your schedule is variable and you don't go to bed and get up at predictable times, there is another "digital" thermostat adjustment device available to you that works reasonably well. And it doesn't cost a thing! In fact, it involves using the digits on your hands.

Even an unsophisticated manual-type thermostat can be made to operate like a programmable one if you remember to set the temperature back every night and dial it up again in the morning. The one drawback is that your house will be cool when you wake up.

For many people, setting a manual thermostat up or down as they leave and enter the house, or go to bed and wake up, becomes a habit that is easy to remember. For others, the automated setback features offered by a digital thermostat make that option more convenient. Digital or manual, the main point is that any time you turn down the thermostat in your house (or turn it up in the summer), you save energy.

WHOLE HOUSE FANS

Whole house fans—boon or bane?

Many homes in the United States have "whole house" fans. These large fans, usually mounted in a top-floor ceiling, are turned on during the summer by homeowners who wish to avoid turning on room air units or a central air-conditioning system—or as an alternative to air conditioning altogether.

The idea behind using a whole house fan is to bring in cooler outside air through open windows while at the same time pushing warmer air through the attic and roof vents. Because of the size of most whole house fans, they are usually effective at accomplishing these tasks. The air movement removes heated air from the attic, which can reduce the heat in the rooms below, and if the incoming air is cooler, then the system does have a cooling effect on the house. Whole house fans can also quickly vent undesirable odors when necessary.

Many people have discovered, however, that air from outside the house often brings with it things they don't want inside, such as humidity, pollen, and dirt. That limits the use of whole house fans at certain times and in some geographical areas, such as states that experience high humidity in the summer.

Whole house fans: Saving energy or wasting it?

Many conventional whole house fan installations lack adequate provision for sealing and insulating the opening in the winter. It is often possible to stand in the attic and see light coming upward through the loose-fitting metal louvers under a whole house fan. Those openings allow great amounts of heated air to escape the house and enter an attic in the winter, resulting in energy waste and higher heating bills. Heat from the attic can also be conducted downward through the opening and the louvers during the warm summer months.

Although a whole house fan can save some energy during the summer by prolonging the periods when a room or central air-conditioning system doesn't run, it can waste energy in the winter by allowing warm air to flow upward through the louvers. Draping a length of fiberglass batt insulation over the fan in the winter—a common practice undertaken to address this issue—is completely ineffective as either an air-sealing or an insulating measure.

Remediation of whole house fans

Several types of commercially available covers are designed to address the issue of air leaking through whole house fan installations. Some mount on top of the fan in the attic; others are simple covers that attach from the house side of the installation and cut down on air leakage. It is also relatively easy to build a lightweight removable cover of fiberglass insulation board or rigid foam board. Sealing these covers is challenging, however, and that is critical to prevent air infiltration.

An alternative to the large conventional whole house fans are the relatively new smaller fans that have spring-loaded, insulated covers that snap tightly into place when the fan is not being used. While they do not move as much air as the larger models, they are effective if used over a longer period of time.

All in all, while many homeowners like and use whole house fans, they do have some serious drawbacks. It is not unusual to find an abandoned fan in the attic with a patched ceiling below. If you already have a whole house fan in place in your home and intend to put it to use, be sure that the opening is sealed and insulated properly during winter. That opening represents one of the largest and potentially leakiest holes in your entire house. Energy that escapes through those leaks will increase your utility bill substantially.

If you're thinking of installing a whole house fan, at least give the smaller-size units a once-over before you make any final decisions. They use less power, seal and insulate better, are quieter, and the hole they require in the ceiling is smaller than that of a conventional unit.

THE FIREPLACE FLUE PIPE

Up the flue

If there were a large hole in your living room ceiling leading directly to the outside of the house, you'd probably notice it and seal it to prevent air from shooting up there. In many homes there is such a hole, but it's hidden inside the fireplace. That hole is the fireplace flue pipe.

Wood-burning fireplaces usually have a damper installed in the upper part of the firebox. The damper is designed to be shut when the fireplace is not in use and can be easily opened when it is. It's common to forget to close the damper after a fire goes out, however, and that leaves a big hole through which heated or cooled air can escape the house.

Even when a fireplace damper is closed, the sealing is often not very effective. Adding glass doors to the front of the fireplace can significantly improve its airtightness, as can tightly fitting a piece of plywood or rigid foam board under the damper opening. Sealing a fireplace flue in this manner can also reduce or eliminate soot odors that are prone to travel into the house during windy or stormy days. Of course, the blocking material must be removed before a fire is started.

One caution, though: Fireplaces with installed gas logs are required to have the damper open at all times. That's either because a pilot light is constantly burning under the logs or because the homeowner might forget to open the damper when he or she turns on the fire. Because gas-log fires produce copious amounts of carbon monoxide, they have to vent outside in a fail-safe manner. That's why there is, or should be, a keep-open device attached to the damper in gas-log fireplaces. Unfortunately, that open damper means house air is running up the flue or cold air might be traveling down.

Another cautionary note: A wood-burning fire must be completely out and the ashes cold before the damper can be shut or other sealing is put into place. The hazard is carbon-monoxide poisoning. A smoldering fire, even though it might not be visible through a layer of ashes, still produces combustion gases. Those gases contain carbon monoxide. Therefore, while it's great to save energy by closing off the damper inside a fireplace, be sure to do so in a safe manner. Do not close a fireplace damper until the fire is completely out.

Shut off the pilot

Gas-log fireplaces are equipped with either a standing pilot light (one that is lit all the time) or with electronic ignition. The electronic-ignition models are much more energy efficient because they burn only when they are turned on.

Standing pilots, on the other hand, burn constantly, wasting a lot of gas when they aren't needed. It is not unusual to find one blazing away in a fireplace during the heat of summer when the probability of someone starting a fire is very remote. If you have a gas-log fireplace with a standing pilot light, consider learning how to shut it off—at least during the summer months. You can start it again in the fall when the weather turns cold and you're more likely to want a fire. Instructions on how to shut off and re-light gas-log pilot lights are printed inside the front panel of most installations or are available from the installer or manufacturer.

FURNACE AND BOILER

Pilot that furnace and boiler

Older gas furnaces and boilers also have standing pilot lights. Unless they're shut off, they burn all summer long. You can save money on your gas bill during the summer by turning off these unneeded standing pilots. Doing so also helps preserve your heating equipment.

One of the by-products of combustion is moisture, and if a standing pilot is left burning in a forced-air furnace over the summer, the moisture produced by the pilot can condense on the inside of the heat exchanger. Coupled with the acids inherent in combustion gases, the mixture can corrode the inside of the heat exchanger, leading to premature rusting, perforation, and failure. This condition is exacerbated if the furnace blower is also used for air-conditioning. The cold air passing through the furnace makes it far more likely that condensation will form inside, shortening the life of the heat exchanger.

ELECTRICITY AND SOLAR ENERGY

Light the way with CFLs

Electricity consumed for lighting typically constitutes just under 10 percent of the household energy budget. One way to reduce that number is to replace frequently used incandescent lights with compact fluorescent light (CFL) bulbs. These long-lasting bulbs use about one third of the power required to produce the same amount of light that is produced by a standard incandescent bulb.

CFLs offer other advantages, too. Standard incandescents give off a substantial amount of heat. Just ask someone who has tried to unscrew a blown bulb with bare fingers after it has failed. That heat, while perhaps welcome in the

Halogen Lights: How Energy Efficient Are They?

Halogen lights require slightly less electricity than standard incandescent bulbs. Some, however, require transformers that suck up power even when the bulbs are turned off.

Halogens also produce a prodigious amount of heat. In fact, they get so hot that they can be fire and burn hazards if installed or used improperly. During the summer that extra heat output is unwelcome and will cause air-conditioning to run more often.

winter, adds to the cooling load during the summer. And a hot bulb is a mark of inefficiency. Any electricity used to produce heat is not going toward the production of illumination. On the other hand, CFLs run cool; they don't contribute to heating load and can be used safely in any fixture that can handle an incandescent—except those controlled by a dimmer switch.

Older versions of CFLs had a few problems, such as unattractively colored light, noise, flickering, and slow start-up. Those issues have largely been resolved in the bulbs currently on the market. The light color is similar to that produced by an incandescent bulb, and electronic ballasts produce flicker-free and noiseless light. Moreover, the new bulbs start right up when switched on—though they may require a few minutes to achieve full brightness. New CFL bulb shapes mean you can put a CFL anywhere an incandescent can go; the bulb shapes have become more compact and "standard-size" over the years.

The price of CFLs has fallen in recent years as well, from double digits to under three dollars each when purchased in multi-packs or on sale. That's still more than incandescents, but with a projected bulb life of as much as 10,000 hours compared to an incandescent's 800–1,000. So in the long run they're a bargain. Plus they save a lot of electricity along the way. An 11-watt model can replicate the light produced by a 60-watt incandescent. That's a savings of 49 watts per hour of operation! Multiply that by the number of lights in your home and their hours of operation, and you'll quickly realize that CFLs are not only the light of the future but also of today.

Daylighting—light tubes

Another way to cut down on the amount of energy consumed for lighting tasks is to increase the use of daylight for illumination. Skylights used to be the only pathway through which natural light could enter rooms near the center of a house. But new products on the market, "light tubes," "sun tubes," or "tubular skylights," have proven to offer many of the benefits skylights bring to the table, and at lower cost.

Light tubes consist of a flexible metal tube that connects a light-gathering dome on top of the house and a light-emitting dome inside the house. Daylight hits the exterior dome and is beamed inside the shiny tube. It bounces around there and comes out through the ceiling-mounted dome. On bright days a light tube can produce more light than a 100-watt bulb.

Because of their modest size and flexibility, light tubes can be installed between standard framing members, requiring no cutting (and thus no re-supporting) of those members. The dome that mounts on the roof is supplied with flashing that integrates with the existing roofing, and the interior dome mounts in a simple hole cut into the ceiling. Because light tubes are not as large as most sky-lights, the heat loss at night is less by comparison.

Although light tubes work only during daylight hours (and not as well on cloudy days), some brands offer op-tional light fixtures inside so the dome can be used at any time of the day or night. Still, these products offer an inter-esting and energy-efficient option for continuous daylight illumination of areas of the home that might otherwise remain dark.

Motion-sensing lights and sensibility
Motion sensors, either built into a light fixture or retrofitted as an add-on to a bulb socket, are usually associated with outdoor applications. And they work well for that purpose. Before motion-sensing lights were invented, homeowners wishing for greater security outside their homes were forced into leaving on outdoor lights all night to illuminate garages, barns, and back doors. That burned up a lot of electricity. Now motion detectors can provide you with illumination when you need it and allow for energy-saving darkness when you don't.

Outdoor lights that come on suddenly due to an activation of the motion sensor can also surprise and thus deter thieves. When someone is caught in the beam of a suddenly illuminated landscape, he or she doesn't know whether the light came on because of a motion sensor or because someone has flicked on a floodlight switch.

Motion-sensing lights can also alert a homeowner that an intruder is passing through a yard. It might only be a neighbor's cat, but sometimes the backyard light suddenly coming on can reveal unexpected occurrences. Virtually any exterior lighting fixture can be upgraded to motion-sensor light status with a simple adapter.

Another benefit to installing motion-sensing lights outside your home is the safety they can provide in lighting your way as you walk to and from your garage. The lights allow you to become aware of any potentially dangerous circumstances and also to illuminate walkways and sidewalks so you can avoid obstructions.

Motion-sensing lights are increasingly making their way inside the home as well. They're handy for places like the landing area at a back door, where you might often enter with your hands full. Closets and pantries are also good candidates for motion-sensor light adapters. You're usually bringing something into or removing something from those areas, so trying to switch on or switch off an overhead light can be challenging. And since the light is only on when you're in those specific areas, the bulb doesn't burn for any longer than necessary—and that saves electricity.

Low-voltage exterior lighting

If you'd like your outdoor landscape to be illuminated at night for safety or for aesthetic reasons, there are ways to do it that don't require much electrical power. One product that is popular for such applications is low-voltage lighting.

While low-voltage lights won't illuminate the entire side of a house or reach to the deepest stretches of a lot like a line-voltage system (120 volts) can, they can guide the way up front steps or along a walkway, or they can accent a landscape feature without making the electric meter spin too rapidly. Another benefit is that, because they are dimmer than line-voltage systems, they don't contribute to light pollution, and neighbors are unlikely to complain that the downward-facing lights keep them awake at night.

LED Holiday Lighting

Light emitting diode (LED) lights are just beginning to transform the way we will light our homes and businesses in the future. These bulbs produce very little heat, burn practically forever, and are highly efficient—as much as 80–90 percent more efficient than incandescent bulbs. LEDs produce a brilliant white light, though the bulbs can also be made with colored glass in order to produce different tints.

You can take advantage of LED technology today in the form of holiday lighting strings. They are available at many hardware stores and home centers. Due to their popularity, however, many places sell out their stock just before the holidays.

So, if your electricity bill skyrockets over the Christmas season due to the use of holiday lighting, consider investing in LED lighting strings to reduce your electrical consumption.

Many low-voltage outdoor lighting systems operate at 12 volts, which makes the installation safe for use when children or pets are around. There is no shock hazard should a wire get cut accidentally. Because the lights can be easily moved around the yard, you can change the display to suit the season, adding or subtracting lights as needed. For even better energy performance, putting the system on a timer turns off the lights when they aren't likely to be needed and on when they are.

Solar-powered landscape lights, which cost nothing to operate, are also available. Installation involves pushing the support stake into the ground. Each light is equipped with a small solar panel on top and a rechargeable battery and bulb inside. The panel charges the battery during the day, and the light stays on all night. Some solar landscape lighting is equipped with bright and high-efficiency LED (light emitting diode) lights for lower energy consumption, durability, and longer-lasting performance.

Don't stand by your power

You probably don't even realize it, but an energy thief is inside your home at this very moment. This thief is silent and unseen, and he's picking your pocket. His name is "standby power."

Standby power is the name given to the electricity used to power electrical appliances and devices even when they are turned off. But how can this be? Isn't an appliance "off" when you switch it off? Not necessarily.

Many electronic devices consume electricity 24 hours a day just to stay warmed up for whenever you decide to use them. "Instant on" TV sets are one example. Whether you watch TV seven hours a day or not at all, the TV is always partially on, staying ready to flicker to life the moment you turn on its switch.

Other devices that consume power constantly are those that have external or internal clocks: microwave ovens, computers, VCRs, DVD players, and cable TV and satellite TV boxes. Energy experts estimate that approximately 5 percent of residential electrical power consumption in the United States is used for standby power. That's a lot of power plants running overtime just to keep our electronics warm and ready to go.

Some of the most prevalent standby power devices are the large plug-in transformers that are used to step down power to cordless phones and answering machines.

How much do these various devices consume? Not much; just a few watts, maybe 3 to 5 each. But multiply that number over a 24-hour day, times the 6 to 10 devices in a typical home, and the scope of the savings could be greater than it may seem.

For many years manufacturers had no incentive to increase the energy efficiency of electronic devices that use standby power. After all, they weren't paying anyone's electric bill. But recently, since more efficient devices have appeared on the market, any electronic equipment you purchase new will likely yield an energy improvement over something that has a few years on it.

A good solution to deal with standby power losses in existing equipment is to plug several of the devices into a power strip that has an on/off switch. Power strips are inexpensive and available at home centers and office supply stores. An entire cluster of items can then be shut off—

really shut off—just by flicking one switch. This works well in areas like home entertainment centers, where a TV, VCR, DVD player, and cable box might already be plugged into one electrical receptacle.

However, if you want to leave some of the devices on—for instance a VCR, to record while you're away, this scheme won't work. And it isn't worth doing on devices that have a clock feature that you depend on to tell time. But if you think it through and separate out devices that can be switched off entirely without consequence, you might be surprised by the number you can put together on one power strip.

Generally speaking, it's a good idea from an energy-efficiency standpoint to unplug anything electronic that you're not using at that moment. Lamps and toasters aren't electronic and don't draw standby power when they're switched off, but battery chargers, TVs, VCRs, DVD players, computers, and stereo systems do. Why pay for this leaking power if you're not using the item?

Set it right
It is surprising how involved we can get with tweaking and adjusting some things in our lives, yet remain utterly oblivious to others. We may spend hours picking out paint for a dining room, yet be unaware that our refrigerators are running too hot or too cold. That can cost money we don't need to spend and consume electricity that does not need to be wasted.

Refrigerator and freezer temperatures can be set using an accurate thermometer and the easy-to-find controls inside the refrigerator compartment. Set the refrigerator to

36 to 38 degrees, and the freezer to 0 to +5. Anything lower than that is wasted. Food won't last any longer if it is kept at a lower temperature, and some items, like lettuce and other vegetables, can even freeze and be destroyed by lower temperatures in the refrigerator compartment, wasting both food and energy.

If you run a dehumidifier in your home, be aware that most are controlled by a humidistat. A humidistat is to humidity what a thermostat is to temperature. In other words, as the humidity in the area where the dehumidifier is running drops to a certain setpoint, the machine will shut itself off until the humidity rises past that setpoint again.

Turning the humidistat to its lowest setting causes the dehumidifier to run constantly, which is wasteful. And because dehumidifiers use quite a bit of electricity, running one as infrequently as possible will benefit your utility bill's bottom line. Finding a humidity level you can live with—and then setting the humidistat to that level—will result in the unit running intermittently, which saves energy compared to one that runs continuously.

MISCELLANEOUS TIPS

Made for comfort

The adjustment to a cooler house in the winter and a warmer one in the summer can be aided by the use of devices designed to increase personal comfort.

As mentioned in the "Live Efficiently" chapter, turning down the house heat and creating your own warmth zone in bed by sleeping under a comforter or an electric blanket saves energy. Small space heaters serve the same purpose in a room setting. If you know you're going to be in one area of the house for a period of time, dialing down the central heating system's thermostat and turning on a space heater in the area where you're located can reduce overall energy consumption during that period. This works well for home offices or entertainment rooms designed for TV or movie watching.

Space heaters don't have to be electric. Gas and wood fireplaces and stoves can also be used in this way. "Ventless" gas fireplaces and kerosene space heaters should be used with caution, as both produce combustion by-products that are released into the air. These heaters are not designed to be a home's primary heat source. Read and follow all directions concerning setup and use of ventless fuel-burning space heaters.

Alternately, in the summer, installing a small room air conditioner in order to cool small areas can reduce your energy bill substantially. Dial up the thermostat in the rest of the house to keep the central air-conditioning system from running so often. The power consumed by a small room air unit is much less than that used by the larger system. This strategy can also be used at night in one or two bedrooms—provided you can sleep with the noise created by a room air conditioner.

GET YOUR HANDS DIRTY

The right techniques and materials can improve the energy efficiency in your house.

- **Cleaning your refrigerator coils and your water heater's tank maintains maximum efficiency.**

- **Caulking leaks in a home not only saves energy but also keeps out insects and other uninvited creatures.**

- **Insulating pipes is not glamorous but is economically beneficial.**

PERIODIC CLEANING IS THE BEST POLICY

Cleaning refrigerator coils

The coils underneath and behind a refrigerator are dust magnets. Refrigerant is pumped and circulated through the coils as a fan blows room air across them. The moving air removes heat from the refrigerant inside the coils. As the fan sucks air from underneath the refrigerator, it brings along with it dust and dirt that stick to the coils. Removing the access panel from the lower front of the refrigerator

Refrigerator Wars

There is now a way to find out how much that old refrigerator or freezer sitting in your garage or basement costs to run every year. Home Energy Magazine has mounted an online searchable database of approximately 85,000 refrigerators and freezers, along with their energy ratings, at: http://www.homeenergy.org/consumerinfo/refrigeration2/refmods.html.

To get the lowdown on your refrigerator you'll need its make and model number—for instance, Amana, TJ18KW. This information can usually be found on a label plate somewhere inside the food compartment or on the front edge of the refrigerator's frame.

After entering the numbers into the site's search engine, the energy ratings will appear on your computer screen. The database lists the date of manufacture, size of the unit, the amount of energy it consumed when it was new, and how much energy it uses at its current age.

For the Amana above, the 17.78-cubic-foot top-freezer model built in 1988 used 856 kilowatt-hours of electricity per year when it was new. In 2005 that amount had climbed to 1,112 kilowatt-hours. At a rate of 10 cents per kilowatt-hour the refrigerator costs $111.20 a year to operate. Since your electrical rate per kilowatt-hour may differ, find the charge on your utility bill.

By comparison, a new 18.4-cubic-foot top-freezer Amana uses only 409 kilowatt-hours of electricity a year—$40.90, an annual savings of $70.30.

can reveal a startlingly filthy sight if the coils haven't been cleaned in a while.

In addition to being unsightly, the dust on the coils acts as insulation that prevents the fan from efficiently removing heat. Cleaning the refrigerator coils a couple of times a year with a vacuum cleaner and an elongated brush helps the refrigerator operate at its maximum efficiency. Moving a refrigerator away from a wall so air can circulate behind it will increase its energy performance, as will keeping it out of direct sunlight and away from heat sources like a radiator or a range.

As energy-saving tips go, cleaning the coils under your refrigerator probably produces little economic effect compared to the amount of effort required to do the job. But it's still a task worth undertaking, if only for the hygienic benefit.

Sediment down the drain

Draining sediment from a water heater's tank is an energy-saving procedure anyone can do quickly and easily. Periodically removing accumulated sediment helps conventional water heaters operate at optimum efficiency. The sediment consists of hard-water minerals and other debris that enter the storage tank along with the incoming water. As the water is heated, the minerals separate from the water and fall to the bottom of the tank.

Over time, the mineral deposits build up to the point that they act as insulation on the bottom of the tank, isolating the water from effects of the burner firing below (on gas and oil units) and sometimes stacking up high enough to cover the heating element on electric water heaters. The harder it is for heat to get through the sediment layer, the longer the burner has to fire or the electric elements have to run in order to heat the water.

The solution is to remove the sediment layer. You do not have to turn off the power source (electricity, gas, or oil) to the water in order to drain the sediment.

A small drain valve is on the outside of the water heater tank's jacket near the bottom. It looks like a miniature hose bibb on the outside of a house. Attach a short length of standard garden hose to this valve, stick the free end of the hose into either a floor drain nearby or a large bucket, and open the valve.

Water will flow from the bottom of the water heater and out the valve and through the hose, taking sediment along with it. After draining five gallons or so from the tank, shut off the valve, disconnect the hose, and empty the bucket (if you used one) into a sink or toilet. You've not only improved the efficiency of your water heater, but you've also extended its service life.

What is the reason? There is a thin film of water that is trapped between the sediment and the bottom of the tank. When the burner fires, the thin layer of water heats to an abnormally high temperature that deteriorates the tank's glass lining, speeding up its rusting process. Accumulated sediment is also responsible for the popping, banging, rumbling, and percolating noises often heard from a water heater as the burner fires or the elements heat up.

Depending on the mineral content of your water, a water heater tank should be drained of its sediment at least twice a year, and more often in hard-water areas.

SEAL THE LEAKS

Lick the envelope

Builders often refer to the exterior of a home as the "envelope" or the "shell." Sealing the envelope or shell against air infiltration (air leaking into the house from outside) and air exfiltration (air leaking from inside the house to the outside) helps reduce your energy expenditure for space heating and cooling. Besides, no one likes to live in a drafty house.

Technicians use a "blower-door test" to accurately measure air leakage in houses. The test involves sealing a portable, frame-mounted fan in an exterior doorway to the house. Any known openings to the outside, such as the fireplace flue; bathroom vent fans; and the flues to the water heater, furnace, or boiler are temporarily sealed.

After the sealing and setup is complete and the blower fan is switched on, it is possible to measure with precision how much air is entering the house through all the various "unintended" cracks, gaps, and holes in the exterior envelope. Using devices called smoke pencils, technicians can pinpoint areas where air is entering the house while the blower door is in operation.

While every home is different and each has its own set of leakage points, there are areas where infiltration shows up repeatedly in blower-door tests. These often include the seam between the top of the foundation wall and the wood framing that runs above, around, and through doors and windows; along baseboards; through electrical receptacles and switches mounted on exterior walls; and around fireplaces, laundry chutes, attic hatchway doors and pull-down stairways, whole-house fan installations, and pipe and wire chases. A homeowner can go a long way toward increasing energy efficiency by locating and sealing up as many of these entry points as possible.

You don't necessarily need to have a blower-door test done on your home in order to locate the unsealed areas that are leaking air. Knowing that these points of air entry have been routinely and consistently identified in other houses gives you a start on where to look for gaps and cracks in yours. A windy day outside can be helpful in this endeavor. Wind can push air into the house through unseen and unnoticed holes to the point that you can feel the air movement.

Pre-OSB

Before plywood and oriented strand board (OSB) were invented, homes were built entirely with solid board lumber. The exterior was sheathed underneath the siding with wide boards that, over time, shrank and cracked. All these cracks—and the many others inherent in most homes—are pathways through which air can enter or leave a house. Sidewall sheathing is covered with siding, so all those cracks that appear in and between wide boards on older homes are hidden and inaccessible.

Air enters the sheathing through cracks in the siding; around windows and doors; and through other openings in the exterior envelope that include kitchen and bathroom vent fan louvers, dryer vents, holes bored for air-conditioning lines, electrical and gas service wires and pipes, along the underside of the lowest course of siding, and through other holes. Any time you can find and seal a crack on the exterior of a house, you go a long way toward reducing air infiltration and exfiltration on the inside.

Because of the large size of plywood and OSB sheets, there are relatively fewer seams in the sheathing on newer homes. And the use of products like house wrap on new construction has further reduced air infiltration . Consequently, most new homes are more airtight than older ones. But although the sheathing might be more airtight in a newer home, there are still many places where air is getting in and out. Finding and sealing those leakage points not only reduces drafts and energy usage, but it also helps keep out insects and other pests.

Block that line (hole)

HVAC system installers need to bore a large hole through the exterior wall of the house in order to pass refrigerant lines through to the compressor outside. Most take time to caulk the hole around the lines, but the caulk fails over time, often leaving a gap where air (and insects) can infiltrate the house. A few minutes spent with a caulk gun will close the gap and shut off the flow of outside air into the house.

Secure the perimeter

The wooden framing in most homes rests on top of a solid concrete or concrete block foundation. In homes built before 1980 or so, the lowest section of wood, called the "mud sill," rests directly on top of the concrete. While the connection is secure from a strength standpoint, in terms of eliminating air infiltration, things could be much better. The problem is the rough and variable surface of the top of

Caulk or Spray Foam—Which to Use Where?

Two of the best products to use in dealing with gaps and holes in your home's envelope are caulk and insulating foam that comes in a spray can.

Acrylic latex caulk can be used on cracks and small openings on the exterior of a home. It can be painted and is durable enough to withstand a moderate amount of expansion and contraction due to weather extremes. It is also useful inside the home to fill gaps around window and door trim on baseboards, as well as to seal up other smaller fissures.

Spray foam is available in two formulations: expanding and nonexpanding. The nonexpanding type is useful for sealing the gaps between window and door jambs in new construction and in other areas as well. Because the foam does not expand, it won't deflect the jambs inward as expanding foam tends to do.

Expanding foam is the product of choice for sealing wiring and holes that run through framing lumber. It is also used for plugging gaps between the top of a foundation wall and the start of the wood framing, around electrical boxes and vent fan housings in attics, and along the tops of room walls that intersect with the attic framing. Expanding foam can fill holes up to about 2 inches in diameter.

the foundation wall. While there are many areas where the wood presses down tightly, other areas may leave a gap through which wind can enter.

The gaps, which collectively might add up to a hole the size of a basketball in the exterior envelope, can usually be sealed with either caulk or cans of spray foam. This procedure, which can be done either on the inside or outside of the house (depending on which offers the best access) requires that you first brush away the dirt and cobwebs from the concrete and wood so the caulk or foam will stick to both surfaces.

From that point on it's just a matter of aiming the caulk tube's tip or spray foam applicator tube at the gaps and gunning them full of caulk or foam. It's a job that doesn't have to be neat or precise, just thorough. Once you're finished, you will have stopped up one of the leakiest places in the home.

In newer homes, the gap between the mud sill and the top of the foundation wall is filled with a thin, compressible length of foam material. The foam creates an airtight seal that does not need remedial caulking or foaming. However, it's worth checking along this area anyway, as occasionally the foam sealer didn't get placed exactly where it should have been. Also, the top of the foundation wall might be too uneven for the foam to fill the gap, someone might have forgotten to put it in place, or it might stop short of the corners. In any of those cases, a shot of caulk or foam can quickly remedy the problem.

Mind the gaps

Some people find that once an older home has been freshly painted, they suddenly feel warmer or "cozier" inside during the winter. That may be because the painter who worked on the house took time to caulk cracks, gaps, and other holes in the home's exterior "skin." While minute gaps around doors and windows might not seem as though they could possibly add up to much, under certain conditions it is surprising how much air they can let into and out of a house.

Consider a windy day. Wind drives air into gaps and around obstructions. Add rain to the mix, and you've got the recipe for both water and air infiltration. So caulking pays off in regard to both energy savings and building preservation. That's why you don't need to wait until it's time to paint to caulk visible openings on the exterior of your house.

Inside move

Once the exterior of the home is sealed as well as possible, it is valuable to do the same to the inside as well. Gaps are often left between baseboards and hard floors, such as tile, hardwood, or laminate flooring. These gaps can be successfully and neatly filled with latex caulk, thus preventing air from entering the home at foot level.

Seasonal wood movement can create cracks around window and door casings; those cracks can also be caulked, preventing air movement in and out of the house. A good tip is to get on a small stepladder and look at the tops of all the door and window casings in the house. Often, these areas are not only unpainted but also uncaulked. It's not unusual to find large gaps between the casing and drywall or plaster. Again, caulk it to seal it.

Infiltration and exfiltration don't only occur between the indoors and outside. Air can move within a house from the basement or the interior rooms up into the attic and beyond. So it's important to caulk around all the interior doors and along the bottom of as much of the interior baseboard as possible.

Attic attack

If you're up for getting a bit dirty, the attic is a good place to engage in some comprehensive and valuable air sealing. The floor of an attic is an important battlefield on the energy conservation front because of a phenomenon known as the "stack effect."

Warm air rises. That much is nearly universally known; it is the reason hot air rises up a fireplace flue or "chimney stack." What isn't so commonly recognized is that rising warm air creates pressure at the top of whatever is containing it. In a household situation the top-floor ceiling acts as a containment barrier to rising warm air. As such, any small hole or gap in that area is subject to pressurized warm air trying to escape.

Warm air loss due to the stack effect has another consequence. As air exits through the top-floor ceiling or other holes, it creates a slight negative pressure inside the house. The air leaving has to be replaced, and that air comes from outside the house: cold, dry air. The incoming air has to be heated, and that's when your furnace or boiler comes on.

Insulation is not air sealing

Most every attic has at least some insulation in it, and that's fine. Insulation helps prohibit heat loss. It doesn't stop airflow, however, and that's a problem. The insulation lying on attic floors often conceals a very large problem—cracks, gaps, and holes through which pressurized air from the house below is driven into the attic.

These fissures take many forms: holes drilled into the wood framing where wiring runs from a room below up into the attic; lighting fixtures and electrical boxes; areas where the tops of partition walls in the room below intersect with the attic-floor framing; bulkheads over kitchen and bathroom cabinets; exhaust vent fans; and fireplace and heating equipment chimneys and flues. It's a long list, and it's likely you can find fissures in your own attic that aren't even mentioned.

Every one of these holes represents an opportunity for warm air to escape the rooms below—and that escaping air represents your energy dollars flying up and away as well. So, although digging through insulation in the attic to find and seal up these trouble spots is probably not anyone's idea of fun, it is time well spent.

The materials used for sealing most attic floor penetrations are caulk and spray foam. The application does not have to be neat; no one is going to come along and grade you on tidy performance. Once you foam or caulk, you'll just cover the area with insulation again. But it will behoove you to do a thorough job. Remember, any gap left unfilled will leak air.

Find 'em and fill 'em

In an attic filled with unfaced fiberglass insulation, it's relatively easy to find spots where air is leaking upward from the rooms below. You'll often see gray, brown, or black smudges or staining in the insulation. Those discolored spots are dirt that was borne on the air leaking from below. Fiberglass insulation strains contaminants out of the air and leaves them there as telltale indicators of air leakage. Lift up the fiberglass batting at one of these spots, and you'll find an opening into the rooms below, maybe an electrical box or wire chase.

Attics insulated with cellulose fiber don't show air-leak smudges. The material is as dark as most airborne dirt, and it doesn't act as a filter. So you'll need to use your sleuthing skills to come up with places likely to contain room ceiling/attic floor penetrations. Examine rooms below before you enter the attic. Take note of where light fixtures and interior walls are located. You may even want to draw a map.

Once you locate a hole that needs to be filled, use a brush to sweep the insulation back, squirt caulk or spray foam to seal the hole or gap, replace the insulation, and move on to the next spot.

Be especially aware that many interior walls have wires running up into the attic. Foam around the wires to fill the holes in the framing. Electrical boxes should have the power switched off before you work around them. Caulking around the box where it penetrates the drywall or plaster and around the wires that run into the box will seal things as well as possible. Vent fan housings can be sealed in a similar manner.

Chimneys require a different approach. Building codes now mandate at least a two-inch gap between any flammable material (usually wood framing) and the masonry or metal. In newer homes this gap is sometimes left unfilled, leaving a hole that goes directly from the basement to the attic. A lot of warm air can rush up a hole that size. Older homes may not have as sizable a gap, but the solution for either is to close the hole with a nonflammable material and fireproof caulk. Sheet metal nailed to the framing and shoved against the chimney works well, and it can be sealed with the caulk to eliminate any of the remaining small gaps.

Pull-down attic stairways

Aside from a whole house fan installation, a pull-down attic stairway probably represents the largest hole in the attic floor—a hole through which a tremendous amount of air can flow in both winter and summer. Some energy experts estimate that the gap around a typical pull-down stairway system can amount to 40 square inches. You'd certainly notice if there was a hole that size in your ceiling, but many people don't connect a pull-down attic stairway with a loss of heat or cooling.

The undersides of many pull-down attic stair units is made of ¼-inch plywood that warps away from its sealing surfaces shortly after installation. Springs that hold the stairway in place lose their resilience over time, allowing the unit to sag down from the opening and further open gaps between the plywood and the jamb. And even in the best of circumstances the entirety of the stair system is uninsulated. It's a worst-case scenario in terms of air sealing and energy efficiency.

Sealing a pull-down attic stairway is tough to do. The stairway, after all, still has to function as an entrance and exit. But adding compressible self-stick foam tape along the upper edges of the plywood door can help reduce air leakage. Adding eyehooks or another type of latching device to the door causes it to jam tight against the foam weather stripping when not in use.

A more comprehensive solution is to insulate the door as well as adding air-sealing capabilities. Several kits are available to solve this dilemma. One is called an "attic tent." It consists of a clothlike material that is caulked and stapled to the framing around the stairway opening. A zipper in the upper part of the tent can be opened for access and closed for air sealing after use. The stairway opens and closes normally underneath the tent fabric. An attic tent, however, provides only a small measure of insulative value compared to the insulation that should be on the rest of the attic floor.

Another kit version is a thick, insulated box that surrounds the stairway opening in the attic. It comes with a removable cover, which can be lifted off when access to the attic is desired, and sealing strips along the bottom of the box that contact either the framing around the stairway or the attic floor. Such a box could also be constructed by a homeowner using rigid foam board and other easily obtainable materials.

Any way you decide to do it, upgrading the air sealing and insulation over a pull-down attic stairway system is an excellent way to invest some time and money. The payback is twofold—better comfort because of fewer drafts and a lower energy bill.

The doorway to stopping air infiltration

While windows attract most of the attention when it comes to energy efficiency, doors can play a major part in what can go wrong—or right. Doors have a particularly difficult role to fill. Not only do they need to open and close smoothly and easily, but they also have to seal tightly to keep out drafts, and must have at least some insulative value to keep cold at bay.

There are many different options on the market that can be used to upgrade a door's existing weather stripping. Some of the most effective are types that contain a vinyl bulb or padded strip set into the edge of a conventional wood doorstop. The wood part is nailed to the doorjamb and is flexible enough to conform to even a badly warped wooden door. The vinyl bulb or strip seals out air movement, but is gentle enough that the door's function is not affected.

Other types of weather stripping include thin bronze or brass strips that are nailed inside the jamb where the door closes. Small nails are driven along one edge of the stripping while the other edge is sprung outward slightly. When the door closes, it contacts the metal strip, bending it a bit and ensuring tight contact with the door edge. This type of weather stripping is time-consuming to install correctly, but it lasts for years and is an effective draft stopper.

Foam tape is usually ineffective as door weather stripping. Even the thinnest foam tape is too bulky to fit along the edge of the doorstop, and if applied in this area, it causes the door to bind and not shut properly. Foam tape is also not durable enough for everyday use in this type of application and soon fails, falling off the doorstop or tearing.

Some contractors are equipped to install a type of vinyl bulb weather stripping that is cut into the door frame with a special tool that resembles a router and cuts a small groove into the intersection of the doorstop and the jamb. A barbed fin on the vinyl bulb weather strip is pressed into the groove, and friction keeps it there. This type of weather stripping is very effective if installed properly, but the hard part is finding someone who has the equipment and know-how to install it.

The threshold of energy efficiency

While weather stripping takes care of weatherizing the top and sides of a door, there's still one edge left to deal with—the threshold. And it's a tough area to address; thresholds accumulate grit and dirt and are subject to a lot of wear and tear. Manufacturers have come up with dozens of solutions to the problem of stopping drafts at the threshold level. Some replacement thresholds are complicated to install. They may require removing the door or even cutting off the bottom of the door. Others are easier to install but don't last long in extreme environmental conditions.

Instead of ripping out the entire old threshold and re-placing it with something new, you may consider installing door bottoms or door sweeps. Door bottoms attach to the bottom of a door and can be adjusted to lightly graze the existing threshold as the door closes.

Door sweeps attach to the inside of the door near the bottom edge—the door does not have to be removed—and consist of a brush or pad that contacts the edge of the threshold as the door shuts. Some doors have a spring-loaded mechanism that snaps the sweep material down as the door closes and retracts it when the door opens, thus creating clearance under the door for an entryway mat. All of these products depend on careful installation to be effective.

On particularly difficult doors to seal, it is worth considering installing a door bottom as well as a door sweep. Much of the draft that gets by the first line of defense will be stopped by the second.

Some doors have adjustable thresholds, but few homeowners make the effort to adjust them as time, settlement, and wear take their toll. It's a good idea every now and then to get down on your hands and knees on the inside of the house in front of an entry door, press the side of your face to the floor, and look at the area where the threshold is supposed to come into contact with the bottom edge of the door. Often you'll see a wide gap; that's where air can breech the door's line of defense.

Adjustable thresholds are usually made from wood or aluminum (sometimes both), and the adjustable part is covered with a removable, replaceable strip of vinyl. After removing the vinyl, you'll see several large screw heads. Those are the adjustors. By tightening or loosening the screws, you can cause the center, adjustable part of the threshold to rise or fall. You'll have to use trial and error to determine how far up or down to move the adjustable portion, but it's worth it to get it right. Once the vinyl strip is back in place, you should not be able to see light coming under the door, and there should be just a little resistance or drag as the door bottom passes over the threshold. If you raise the threshold too far and create too much drag, both the door bottom and the vinyl strip will wear out prematurely.

Older doors equipped with vinyl door bottoms and adjustable thresholds may suffer from torn or worn parts. While some generic replacement parts are usually available at hardware stores and home centers, the best bet for a perfect match is to contact the original manufacturer of the door.

Storm doors

Storm doors, like storm windows, can add draft-stopping ability, insulation, and protection to a home's entry doors. The better the installation and the tighter the fit of a storm door, the more effective it will be. Aluminum storm doors have frames that screw to the outside of the door casing. There might be gaps between the frame and the casing, and those can be filled with caulk.

Another area of potential air infiltration is the door bottom. Most storm doors have an adjustable door bottom that can slide up or down once the screws holding it in place are loosened. This adjustability allows the door bottom to fit snugly to the door's threshold.

There is usually a vinyl strip that seals the storm-door bottom to the edge of the threshold, and those sometimes get torn or worn out. Replacements are available but are sometimes difficult to track down. Similarly, the weather stripping that is attached to the frame and contacts the face of the door as it closes must also be in good condition for the storm door to function as it was designed.

When a storm door is properly sealed and adjusted, it will make the prime door on the house slightly difficult to close. With no other place to go, air trapped between the two will have to rush out around the sides, top, and bottom as the prime door shuts. And when opening the prime door, the storm door should suck in slightly as air is pulled out of the area between the doors. When that happens, you know you've done just about everything that can be done to make a storm door as effective as possible.

A canister of trouble

Recessed ceiling canister lights pose special problems for a homeowner bent on making a home more energy-efficient. The older types are extremely leaky and are difficult to make airtight. Because of regulations concerning fire safety, the best you can do is to build an airtight box of flame-resistant material—sheet metal, for instance, or drywall—at least three inches larger than the light's housing to cover the portion of the fixture that is in the attic. This box can then be sealed to the drywall. It cannot be covered with insulation, however, as heat buildup inside the fixture could cause problems with the wiring inside.

Heat generated by the bulbs inside recessed canister lights is usually lost to the attic and doesn't contribute to heating the house. This excess heat flowing unchecked into the attic space can cause problems with ice dams in the winter.

Another solution to older, leaky canister lights is to replace the fixtures entirely with new airtight units. "ICAT" (insulation contact, airtight) canister lights are the most energy-efficient recessed canister lights on the market. As the name suggests, they are airtight and can also be covered with insulation. To further improve their performance, airtight ceiling canister lights can also be sealed to drywall or plaster with caulk. When you calculate the cost of allowing heat to escape through a leaking ceiling canister light, the cost it takes to replace it with a more energy-efficient model is easy to justify.

Batten the hatches

Instead of a pull-down stairway system, most homes have a small, hatchlike attic-access opening in the top floor ceiling often concealed in a closet. This opening deserves careful examination, as the way attic-access scuttleholes are usually constructed leaves open the potential for air leakage.

Many homes have hatches that consist of a warped sheet of ¼-inch plywood resting on ill-fitting wood pieces nailed to the ceiling framing. The gaps between the plywood and wooden stops are often large enough to push your fingers through. The pressurized warm air lying along your ceiling is just waiting to escape through those gaps.

A better, more energy-efficient attic hatch can be made out of flat ¾-inch plywood with several inches of rigid foam board glued to the back. The tops of the wooden stops where the hatch cover rests can be upgraded for better air-seal ability with self-stick compressible foam tape and where gaps between the stops and framing can be caulked. As a further upgrade, the hatch can be fitted with eyehooks that snug it down against the foam, assuring the foam's compression and a more airtight seal.

Insulation upgrading

These days most attics already have some insulation lying on the floor, but most homes don't have enough insulation up there or have insulation that isn't working as well as it should be. An upgrade—one that will pay off every year and in every season you live in your home—is only one messy afternoon away. Yes, you can and should add more insulation to your attic. It's one of the best ways to increase your home's energy efficiency.

R-factor is a numerical indicator of an insulation's efficiency at retarding the flow of heat. The scale goes from low to high; higher R-numbers mean a given insulation is better able to stop heat from moving from one place to another. Current building codes recommend an insulation R-factor of R-38 for attics in most of the country. That would be about 10-12 inches of fiberglass batting or blown cellulose fiber insulation. Bear in mind that R-38 is actually the minimum recommended standard for attic insulation. Proposed energy codes would increase that number to R-50.

Fiberglass and cellulose fiber are the two most common attic insulation materials. Each yields an R-factor of roughly 3.5 per inch. Cellulose consists of ground-up newspaper material, which is then treated with fire-retardant chemicals. Fiberglass is made of billions of strands of extruded glass fibers packed into specifically sized batts. Some fiberglass batting now comes encased in perforated poly bags to help contain loose glass fibers and make handling and installation easier. Fiberglass also is available as a loose-fill or blown-in material.

While it is possible to do a good job fitting and installing fiberglass batting around all the many framing members and other obstructions in an attic, it is somewhat rare to see such a thorough installation. Many homeowners and insulation installers either don't understand the importance of tightly fitting the material into the many spaces that abound in an attic or find the job too tedious to do correctly. Usually there are gaps and holes between batts and between batts and framing. Those holes defeat much of the insulative value the material can provide.

Cellulose fiber, on the other hand, because it is ground into a fine material, flows and can be blown into all the attic's nooks and crannies, allowing it to do a better, more comprehensive insulation job. And nearly any determined homeowner can do it. Home centers that sell insulation of all types even loan insulation blowers to customers who buy a certain number of bags from their stores. Information on how to operate the machines and install the insulation is available in those stores and from manufacturers.

Cellulose fiber insulation is also less subject than open fiberglass to what builders call "wind wash," which is simply air currents moving through insulation, robbing it of its R-value. Fiberglass batts that are enclosed in perforated poly bags are less subject to wind wash than are either open batts or loose-fill fiberglass insulation.

Any type of attic insulation can be installed over any other type: fiberglass over cellulose, cellulose over fiber-glass—it makes no difference. The fiberglass must be unfaced, however, or encased in perforated poly bags. Otherwise, condensation could develop on the facing.

If your attic has a floor and is used for storage, the potential insulation depth is limited by the depth of the floor joists. Thus, many attics could have a substandard R-factor of only 20 or so—unless you go to the trouble of removing the floor and adding additional framing lumber to the tops of the joists and then reinstalling the floor.

An easier solution than floor removal is to consolidate the stored items into a smaller area (or remove them from the attic entirely), and roll out poly-encased fiberglass batting on top of the floor. The batts can be removed or rolled back at any time if the space is required for storage in the future.

While the price of fuel oil, gas, and electricity continues to rise, attic insulation is relatively inexpensive and remains one of your best energy-efficiency upgrade values.

Sidewall insulation

Homes lose heat through their sidewalls as well as through their attics. Many older homes, built before sidewall insulation had been invented or perfected, are candidates for this upgrade. Measured in square footage, the sidewalls in most houses represent the largest exposure of any area to the outdoors. So it makes sense to make them as resistant to heat flow as possible.

Several different materials can be used for sidewall insulation: cellulose fiber, fiberglass, and a number of different types of foam. Each will not only retard heat flow from the inside of the house to the outside but will also cut down on air infiltration through gaps in the sheathing and other areas. Some foam products can be injected into sidewall cavities even if there is already insulation in place.

While sidewall insulation can be installed from inside the house through holes drilled into plaster or drywall, the usual protocol is to do it from the outside. This tricky job is best left to the experts.

Injection holes can be drilled through wooden clapboard siding and then plugged with paintable plastic caps, or some lengths of the siding can be removed and then replaced after holes have been drilled through the sheathing. Holes in stucco-sided homes can be patched with stucco-cement materials, and vinyl and aluminum siding can be temporarily removed and then replaced after the insulation-installation process is complete.

Weathering the storms

Storm windows can play a key part in your energy-saving plans. They act as a wind buffer, and the air trapped between the storms and the prime windows acts as insulation. In addition, storm windows protect the prime windows from the weather, which can extend the time between paint jobs required on the house.

Older homes are often equipped with heavy wooden storm windows that need to be put up in the fall and taken down in the spring when they are usually replaced with wooden-framed screens. Newer options, and a worthy upgrade to wooden storm windows, include permanently installed aluminum or vinyl storms, which self-store the window glazing and screens. Instead of lugging large storm windows up and down a ladder twice a year, you can simply open each prime window from the inside and slide the glazing or screen portions up or down. This reconfigures the storm window depending on the season.

Many people choose to remove the lightweight screen portion of the storm window during the winter, preferring to look only through window glass instead of screening. Not only is the window glass more aesthetically pleasing, but without a screen in place sunlight can also shine more directly into the house, allowing you to benefit from solar heating.

Another advantage to having storm windows installed on your house is that the extra layer of glazing cuts down on neighborhood and traffic noise. And storms keep out dust and dirt that otherwise might filter in through leaky prime windows.

Temporary window sealing

Owners of older homes that still have their original windows are often dismayed by the amount of cold air leaking through those old windows during the winter. There are several ways of dealing with this problem that don't involve a lot of time or money. One involves using a caulk gun and "weather stripping caulk sealant" or "temporary" caulking to seal up the cracks between the window and window frame. Weather stripping sealant is caulk that is designed to stick in place nearly as well as regular caulk but can be peeled off when it is no longer needed. It is available inexpensively in regular caulk tubes and comes in a clear color. It is nearly invisible when in place and removes easily without damaging either paint or clear finishes.

One drawback to temporarily caulking windows is that once the caulk is in place, the window can't be opened without destroying the seal. This could pose a problem if, for instance, there is a day when you'd like to open the windows to take advantage of a warm breeze. Of course, you could peel the caulk off and then reapply it when the weather turns cool again. But it's better to wait until you're sure there will be no more warm days.

Several lightweight plastic, disposable, interior "storm window systems" are also on the market and are effective in keeping out cold drafts and increasing the insulative value of a window assembly. These kits consist of double-stick tape that is applied to the trim casing around the window, and lightweight plastic sheeting that is pressed onto the tape. Once the plastic is in place, a hair dryer is blown across the surface of the sheeting, causing the plastic to shrink and remove the wrinkles. Like caulking windows shut, this system is best used once you're pretty sure you won't be opening the windows for a couple of months.

While plastic interior storm window kits are effective in helping to prevent heat loss through windows, they are noticeable and might look out of place in formal areas of your home.

Don't blow a gasket

Wind can sneak in through tiny gaps and cracks that you don't even know are there. Often, the first time you're aware of such a problem is when you flick a switch or plug an electronic device into a receptacle mounted on an exterior wall. Not only does the switch or receptacle feel cold, but it's sometimes possible to actually feel a cold draft blowing into the room.

The problem lies outside the house: it's the hole that allows the wind into the house in the first place. But you can block many of these types of drafts from inside the house by purchasing and installing inexpensive switch and receptacle gaskets from a hardware store or home center. The gaskets, made of nonelectrically conductive fiber matt material, fit snugly around the switch or receptacle after the cover plate is removed. With the gasket in place the standard cover plate goes back on, creating an airtight seal against the wall. For the cost of just a few cents each, gaskets are a worthwhile investment in energy saving and comfort.

One caution: To avoid electrical shock, you should remove cover plates from switches and receptacles only after power has been shut off at the main service panel to the circuits where work is being done. Other than that, each gasket installation will require about two minutes of your time.

The garage/house interface

Homes with attached garages often have "interface" problems that can lead to waste of heat and cooling. Because the garage is attached to the house, in many cases the effort that goes into sealing the outside of the house against the weather is not extended to the garage. That's a mistake, because in the winter the garage can become just as cold as the outdoor air—and in the summer, even hotter than it is outside.

There are often holes in garage walls, either put there intentionally or accidentally, that allow air movement between the two areas. Not only are these potential pathways for heated or cooled air to escape or infiltrate, but they are also a danger.

The shared wall between a house and garage is required to be fire-rated. That's so a fire that starts in the garage will be contained there for as long as possible before it breaks through to the house. Garage fires are more common than many people think; car batteries develop short circuits, and gasoline is often stored in cans for use with lawn mowers and other yard maintenance equipment. A hole in a wall between a garage and house can compromise fire safety.

There is another hazard that can involve a leaky shared garage and house wall. That has to do with carbon monoxide. An automobile produces a tremendous amount of carbon monoxide gas, especially when its engine is cold, as it is when first starting up. If you start your car in the garage in the morning and then pull it outside, shutting the garage door traps a large volume of carbon monoxide inside. This deadly gas can leak or be pulled into the house if there are pathways in the shared wall that allow it to infiltrate.

The solution is to make every effort to seal up areas where air might be able to pass between the house and garage. Prime locations are the bottom of the wall inside the garage and the bottom of the doorway into the house. There is a juncture between the framing and concrete where the bottom of the wall meets the concrete foundation that is similar to the one around the perimeter of the rest of the house. This location sometimes lacks a layer of compressible foam between the two materials that would provide an airtight seal. Caulk or foam applied either inside the basement (as previously described in the section on sealing this seam) or in the garage can effectively seal the gap.

It is also worth using caulk or foam to seal the bottom edges of the drywall to the concrete. The reason? In negative pressure situations, air can be drawn into this crack or into the stud cavities inside the wall, and then it can enter the house via an electrical receptacle in that wall inside the house. For instance, negative pressure can occur when the kitchen vent fan is running. That forces air out of the house, and as a result the atmospheric pressure inside the house decreases. The pressure seeks to equalize by drawing air into the house through any opening it can. If the path of least resistance happens to be that crack along the bottom of the garage/house wall, the incoming air can bring carbon monoxide along with it. Adding gaskets to receptacles on both sides of the wall also helps in keeping contaminated garage air out of the house.

The door into the house from the garage is often a leak point as well. Caulking around all the trim and an examination of the door's weather stripping to ensure that it is intact will help block off this potential air passageway. The door bottom must contact the threshold in the way it was designed to do in order to keep air out. Frequently used doors like the one from the garage into the house might need repair or replacement of the weather stripping more frequently than do other entry doors.

Up the flue

Builders occasionally run into difficulty framing and sealing an opening around a fireplace. There needs to be clearance between the wood and the masonry or metal, so the framing can't fit tightly against those materials. That means the finish wall material—usually drywall or plaster—is supposed to bridge the gap for fire safety and also provide an airtight closure. Comprehensive sealing in this area, however, can sometimes be neglected. In some cases that means there are gaps around fireplaces that allow air to leave the house easily.

Take time to look inside and around fireplaces with a good flashlight to see whether there are any holes and gaps that need to be sealed with spray foam, fireproof caulk, or other filler material. Not only will this reduce the amount of air leaving the house via these pathways, but it can also protect areas from sparks or embers leaping out of a fire.

BENEFICIAL LANDSCAPING

The exterior buffer zone

Many opportunities to configure the landscape outside a house can help save energy inside. One good idea is to plant trees along the side of your property that faces the prevailing wind. Anything you can put in the path of a wind is beneficial: a fence, trees, shrubbery. Blocking the wind reduces the amount of heat swept off that side of the house, and it can also help reduce drafts if you can't get to or haven't found all the areas where air is infiltrating the exterior envelope.

Trees can play a big part in reducing cooling expenses in the summer. The shade from a large tree reduces the temperature of the air surrounding a house by an average of ten degrees, and it can block sunlight from penetrating where it is not wanted. The cooler the air outside the house, the less temperature differential the A/C system has to maintain with the inside air.

Deciduous trees are especially valuable, for they block the sun's unwanted rays during the summer, yet drop their leaves and allow sunlight into the house during the winter.

PLUMBING INSULATION AND WATER CONSERVATION

Pipe wrappers

What does pipe insulation do? It keeps heat inside the pipes where it belongs, rather than radiating out into the air. The result is that hot water reaches distant bathrooms faster than it would otherwise, reducing the volume of water that has to flow down the pipe for hot water to effectively arrive. And once hot water fills the pipe, it stays there for a long time. So if you use a hot water tap again shortly after the first usage, it's likely that the water will still be sufficiently hot.

In addition, pipe insulation helps reduce "standby" heat losses at the water heater. Standby heat losses occur while the water heater is just sitting there doing nothing at all. Over a period of time, heat radiating from the water heater's tank and the pipes entering and exiting the top of the unit reduce the temperature of the water inside the tank. Eventually, the thermostat is activated and the burner fires or the electric elements switch on. The water heats up again, only to cool down gradually through the cooling effects of the tank and pipes. It's an endless cycle, exacerbated by the heat loss through the pipes at the top of the water heater. So, although the hot water pipes are the logical ones to insulate, insulating the first five feet or so of the cold water pipe at the water heater is a good idea, too. That helps reduce the loss of heat that migrates up the pipe from the water heater tank.

Although insulating the pipes at the water heater might eliminate only one burner firing or element activation a day, at today's gas and electric prices, that can add up to substantial savings over the course of a year.

It may also be worthwhile to insulate another cold water pipe in your house—the water service entry pipe from a municipal supply or well—though not for energy-efficiency reasons. Throughout the winter and into the spring, water coming into the house through that pipe is cold. If the air is humid enough, condensation can form on the outside of the pipe and drip down onto carpets, suspended ceiling tiles, and anything else along its path. Covering the exposed pipe with foam insulation isolates the pipe from the humid air, preventing condensation from forming.

Insulating water pipes used to involve a large roll of itchy fiberglass insulation, a lot of time, and a lot of cutting and fitting the wrapping around obstructions. And even after all that work, the insulation was so thin that it didn't do much good. Insulating the water pipes in your home these days is simpler, quicker, and more effective.

The closed cell foam pipe insulation available at plumbing supply houses and home centers not only insulates far better than the old fiberglass material, but it's also easy to install. Each piece is slit along its length, allowing the insulation to simply snap over the pipe. The foam is so soft that it can be cut with a kitchen knife or a pair of heavy scissors.

Water heaters—Beefing up the insulation

New water heaters are being built with better insulation these days, so if you have an old unit, don't be shy about adding an extra layer of insulation. There are water heater "blankets" available at home centers and hardware stores that wrap the exterior of the unit with an additional layer of insulation.

Electric water heaters can be covered top to bottom with insulation. Gas water heaters, however, must not be covered on top or along the bottom. The top contains the flue, and that can get hot enough to ignite flammable materials.

The bottom must be left open so air can enter the burner assembly for proper combustion of the natural gas, propane, or oil.

The end of the pressure and temperature relief valve extension pipe (usually running down the side of the unit) on any type of water heater must be left open and exposed as well. This pipe has to be free of obstructions in case the valve activates and releases hot water or steam. Any blockage could interfere with the free release of the pressure within the tank, and that could be dangerous.

Other than that, the more insulation you can wrap around a water heater, the fewer "standby" losses will occur, the less the burner or elements will come on, and the more efficient it will be overall. This is a relatively easy and inexpensive task that pays off every hour of every day from the moment you put the blanket on. Like most jobs involving insulation, it's not glamorous, but it works.

Reduced-flow showerheads

Nearly half of all water used in a home is used for bathing. Almost all of that water needs to be heated. Therefore, the bathroom is an ideal place to practice energy and water conservation. Since January 1995, showerheads in new homes have been required to dispense no more than 2.5 gallons per minute. If you have a showerhead older than that in your home, it takes but a few minutes to replace it with a showerhead that meets the modern flow rate standards.

Showerheads aren't expensive. Ten to twenty-five dollars will purchase a new one that meets the 2.5-gallon limit. If you have an older showerhead that allows up to 6 gallons a minute and subsequently install a low-flow showerhead, you'll reduce your shower water use by more than three gallons per minute.

Water entering a home in northern states in the winter can be as cold as 38 degrees. Heating water that cold to the 120 degrees or so needed to produce a reasonably hot shower demands quite a bit of energy. So it's easy to understand why taking advantage of 2.5-gallon showerhood technology can save a lot on your utility bill.

A caveat though: Putting a low-flow showerhead into use is not an excuse to spend more time in the shower. In some cases, the length of time a person spends in a shower is exactly equivalent to how long the hot water in the water heater's tank lasts. Once the hot water runs out, the shower is over. If it took, say, ten minutes to exhaust your water heater's capacity with a six gallon per minute showerhead, does that mean you can now stay under the running water for 20 minutes with a reduced-flow shower-head in place? Technically, yes. But that would result in no energy or water savings. If you confine your shower activities to simply washing, rinsing, and then getting out, keeping the shower's length the same as it was before the introduction of the new showerhead, you'll decrease your use of energy and water.

Faucet aerators

Older-style bathroom and kitchen sink faucets can deliver as much at 3.5 to 5 gallons of water per minute. Much of that water is wasted; typical washing tasks can usually be accomplished using less.

Faucet aerators, either supplied on new faucets or as inexpensive retrofit add-ons to older faucets, reduce the flow rate to 0.5 to 1.0 gallon per minute in bathrooms, and 1.0 to 2.0 gallons per minute at the kitchen sink. Because air is added to the water stream at the faucet's tip, the flow seems full although the actual volume of water is substantially reduced. This allows you to do more with less hot water.

FURNACE AND AIR-CONDITIONING

Filter replacement

The filter on a forced-air furnace performs a valuable function in the home. It strains bits of dust, dirt, and debris from the air stream as it passes through the furnace. This not only improves air quality, but it also protects the inside of the furnace (and air-conditioning evaporator coil, if there is one). Without a furnace filter in place, dirt would build up on the back side of the heater exchanger and inside the evaporator coil. That dirt would act as insulation and interfere with the efficient transfer of heat from the furnace or cooling from the air conditioner to the air passing through it.

But a furnace filter also slows the passage of air through the furnace—especially when it is dirty. The best way to keep your furnace operating at its maximum efficiency is to keep a clean filter inside. That's one of the only things you as a homeowner can do to maintain your furnace. Filters can be purchased in bulk and replaced every 30–45 days, or they can be vacuumed at those same time intervals.

People who own pets may find that their furnace filters need to be replaced or cleaned more frequently, due to pet dander, hair, and dirt brought in from outside.

It is important to remember that in most homes that have a central air-conditioning system, the furnace's blower is used to distribute cool and dehumidified air during the summer months. Therefore, air passes through the furnace—and the furnace filter—during those months as well. That's why homeowners with central air-conditioning systems need to change or clean filters in the summertime at roughly the same intervals as they do during the winter. The more freely air can pass through the furnace, the more heat and cooling it can distribute while wasting less energy.

Name that tune

Furnaces, boilers, and air-conditioning systems all have mechanical, moving parts in addition to electrical components. Over time these parts can go out of adjustment and need lubrication and cleaning. Like an automobile, your heating and cooling equipment runs best when it is "tuned up" and all the parts are working together as they were designed.

Tuning up HVAC equipment, especially the newer, more complicated systems, should be attempted only by service people who have the training and the equipment to do the work. How often should you call for service? For oil-fired systems, the recommended interval is a year. Gas-fired furnaces and boilers and air-conditioning systems should be checked at least every two years.

Just as tuning up a car can yield better gas mileage, the money you spend on servicing your HVAC equipment will pay off in better efficiency—and will also extend the life of the components.

Finny monsters

Hot water baseboard and electric baseboard heating systems run at maximum efficiency only if the baseboard convectors and radiators are kept clean. These systems depend on air flowing through the many fins that surround the pipes or heating elements. Obstruction of that air—either from dirt and dust buildup or from something covering the top or bottom of the heating units—compromises the performance of the entire system. As is the case with a forced-air furnace, freely flowing air contributes to better efficiency and energy conservation.

Removing or opening the covers that surround baseboard convectors exposes the fins that distribute heat from hot water inside the pipes or heating elements. Vacuuming and brushing the fins, and straightening any that are bent, ensures efficient airflow—and thus efficient heat transfer to the air.

Duct sealing

A startling statistic: Professional heating, ventilation, and air-conditioning organizations estimate that 25 percent of the air traveling down a poorly installed forced-air duct system winds up somewhere other than where it was intended to go. In other words, some duct systems leak 25 percent of the air passing through them. That leakage might occur in basements, crawl spaces, duct chases, or attics. The bottom line is that you're not getting all the heating and cooling for which you are paying.

The solution to leaky ducts is duct sealing. While it is tempting to use a product called "duct tape" to do this job, regular duct tape is actually poorly suited for duct sealing. The adhesives in cloth duct tape break down in the presence of heat; eventually the tape fails and falls off the duct.

A product better suited for the task is duct-sealing mastic, available in tubs at heating supply houses, hardware stores, and home centers. To apply duct mastic, dip a gloved hand into the tub, scoop out some mastic, and smear it all around every single joint you can find in your ductwork. The mastic has the consistency of pancake batter, and once it cures it stays on the duct and doesn't leak.

There are plenty of opportunities in most forced-air heating and cooling systems to upgrade the performance of the ducts. Loosely fitting joints and gaps large and small should be sealed as soon as possible.

After a sealing job is complete, diverter vanes inside the ducts (if they are installed) might have to be rejiggered because air that was supposed to go to a certain area will finally be doing so. The result might be that a formerly cold room is suddenly the warmest one in the house. Also, the furnace or A/C compressor might not come on as often once the conditioned air is getting to where it was designed to go. Duct mastic is inexpensive, the time it takes to seal up your ducts is minimal, and the results can be dramatic.

Duct wrappers
After duct sealing is complete, it's time to think about upgrading your forced-air delivery system even further. Any ducts passing through unheated crawl spaces or attics should be insulated. Heat and cooling thrown off by the

ducts in such areas is completely wasted, but if that heat and cooling were retained, the furnace or air conditioner might not have to work so hard to condition the house.

Duct insulation is available in both wrapping and sleeve types. Sleeves are more effective because they have fewer seams, but may require temporary disassembly of the ducts in order to slip them into place.

Hot water boiler pipes

Distribution pipes in water-heating systems benefit greatly from an insulation wrap. With insulation in place, hotter water gets to the radiators or convectors, increasing the efficiency of the entire system. In addition, less heat is lost to the areas through which the distribution pipes run. Closed-cell foam insulation is available in many sizes at heating supply stores.

Refrigerant line insulation

The flexible lines that shuttle refrigerant from an outside air-conditioning compressor and the evaporator coil in the furnace have insulation on them at the time of installation. Over the years the insulation deteriorates, especially outside the house where it is exposed to sun and temperature extremes. Removing old, torn refrigerant line insulation and replacing it with new material is a good way to ensure that the cold emanating from the pipe isn't lost to the atmosphere outside the house.

Clear and comb a path to the A/C

Air-conditioning systems work by moving refrigerant from inside the house to outside. Inside the furnace evaporator coil, the refrigerant absorbs heat from the air passing through the blower compartment. The refrigerant is then pumped outside and flows into a heat-transfer assembly called the condenser. The condenser coils resemble an automobile's radiator. As refrigerant flows through small tubes in the condenser coils, thin metal fins attached to those tubes extract heat from the refrigerant.

A fan inside the condenser moves air past all the tiny fins and tubes, accelerating the transfer of heat from the refrigerant to the outside air. But this cooling flow of air can take place only when the pathways to the compressor are unobstructed. Landscape plantings, ivy, decks, or benches built over and around the compressor restrict the free flow of air through the system, reducing its efficient transfer of heat. So, to get the most for your A/C dollar, it's a good idea to keep the outside compressor unit cleared of nearby obstructions.

Because airflow through the condenser is important for the efficient function of a central air-conditioning system, carefully examine the outside of the condenser unit from time to time. The thin metal fins are fragile and can bend if something comes in contact with them—a baseball, lawn mower tire, or edge of a rake, for example. "Fin combs" are inexpensive at heating supply stores and home centers, and they can straighten several rows of bent fins at once.

MAKE IMPROVEMENTS AROUND THE HOUSE

When you upgrade your heating and cooling equipment, appliances, and windows, you are investing in energy efficiency.

- **Learn how spout (AFUE) ratings affect your heating bills.**

- **Get a furnace that draws combustion air from the outside.**

- **Invest in a tankless water heater: You'll never run out of hot water.**

WEIGHING COSTS AND SAVINGS

Wise purchases result in financial benefits

Although you can do many free or inexpensive things in and around your home to upgrade its energy efficiency, there are times when purchasing or upgrading something in

order to save money on your utility bill can make sense.
Think of this as "investing in energy efficiency."

Here's an example: If your refrigerator is 15 years old
or older, replacing it with a new one could reduce your
energy bill by five dollars or more every month: 60 dollars a year. If that new refrigerator costs $600, you're
getting a 10 percent return on your money—much more
than banks are paying on savings, checking accounts, or
even certificates of deposit. And the extra bonus is that
money "earned" on energy savings isn't subject to state or
federal income tax. A 10 percent, tax-free return on a moderate investment? That beats leaving potentially savings-
producing money like this in a bank account (where returns
are low—and also taxed).

When you invest money and time in projects like upgraded attic insulation and better air sealing, the benefits
begin immediately and keep paying off every day for the
life of the house. You may save hundreds of dollars in
utility bills.

Figuring out the heating payback

You've heard and read all the stories in the news about
rising energy prices, and you're wondering if buying a new
furnace, boiler, or air-conditioning compressor is worth the
money. The short answer is that the higher energy prices
go, the shorter "payback" time you'll see if you do decide
to purchase new and more efficient heating and cooling
equipments.

The longer answer is that it is impossible to put a firm
dollar figure on exactly how much you might save by upgrading. There are too many variables—the most important

(and lately the most volatile) being the fluctuating price of heating fuel. Geographical location is also a very important factor—and how the seasonal weather situation shapes up in your section of the country—as is how frugally you already live in your home.

Calculating what you pay now

To get a quick read on some of the potential savings you could realize by upgrading your heating and cooling equipment, you can do a calculation using your previous utility bills. Though crude (and based on any fluctuation from the previous year's fuel costs), it will, at least, give you an idea about how much you could save and whether the expenditure is worth considering in your particular circumstance.

The first task is to find out how much you spent on gas and electricity the previous year during the months when you weren't typically using gas, oil, or electricity to heat or cool your home. Your lowest utility bills of the year will usually be in the spring and fall. Find a few bills from these months and average them together to come up with a "typical" no-heating and no-cooling expense month. This will give you a "base load" figure. In other words, this is what you typically spend every month for water heating, cooking, clothes drying, lighting, and other uses that do not involve turning on the major heating and cooling equipment.

Multiply the base load figure by 12, and the sum is your yearly base load rate for gas, oil, and electricity.

Next, add up an entire year's worth of bills; say from December of one year to December of the next year. Subtract the yearly base load rate from the yearly total bill, and what is left over is what you spent on heating and cooling during that year. You can further refine the process by breaking down the calculations into separate gas, oil, or electricity categories.

With these numbers in hand, you'll be better able to decide whether or not it makes sense to upgrade to higher-efficiency mechanical equipment.

Efficiency ratings—what do they mean?

Furnaces and boilers are categorized by their "annualized fuel-utilization efficiency" rating, or AFUE. You'll see those rating numbers, expressed in percentages, when you research heating equipment or talk to a contractor about having new equipment installed.

As an example of how the AFUE ratings could have an effect on your heating bill, say your present forced-air gas furnace is 15 years old and is operating at about 75 percent efficiency (considered to be standard for that era). Your utility bill for the entirety of last year was $2,000. Your base load rate for gas and electricity was $80 per month, or $960 for the year. That means you spent about $1,040 to heat and cool your home last year ($2,000 for the entire year's bills minus $960 base load).

Of that $1,040 about 70 percent, or $728, was spent on natural gas, while $312 was for electricity. So, it cost approximately $728 to heat your home last year.

If you have a 95-percent-efficient furnace installed to replace your 75-percent model, you should save about 20 cents per gas-heating dollar or about $146 over the course of one year. Since super-high-efficiency furnaces cost about $1,000 more than the standard units, it would take almost seven years to pay that amount back based on energy savings alone ($1,000 divided by $146 equals 6.8 years).

However, here's the big variable that calculation does not take into account: increasing gas prices. We now know that global atmospheric and political conditions can throw even the best price predictions for a loop. If fuel prices increase, the savings will be larger and the pay-back time shorter. And even if gas prices don't go up, a tax-free "return" of about 5 percent per year (say, $3,000 for a new furnace, yielding about $146 in energy savings a year) isn't too shabby an investment. Also, the blower-fan motors in new furnaces use electricity more conservatively, so you'll reduce electrical consumption, contributing to the savings.

Homeowners who live in colder locations use more heating fuel and thus can realize faster payback periods. Those who live in climates that require more cooling than heating will benefit more from high-efficiency air-conditioning units than they would investing in higher-efficiency heating equipment.

In the United States, about 75 percent of residential heating is delivered through forced-air systems, and the average age of those furnaces is 17 years, while 25 percent are more than 20 years old. Since the average yearly utility bill is about $1,500, there is reason to consider an upgrade if you have an older furnace. Here are some details about how furnaces operate, and why the newer ones are more efficient.

REPLACING THE FURNACE AND BOILER

Furnaces

From the 1950s through the early 1980s, most furnaces had AFUE efficiency ratings of about 65 percent. That meant approximately 35 percent of the heat the furnace produced was lost up the fluepipe. Over the last couple of decades the AFUE rating of all furnaces has risen to the point that some boast 97-percent efficiency.

Currently, national standards require that furnaces yield a minimum of 78-percent efficiency. It is possible to purchase one with nearly any efficiency rating between 78 percent and 95 percent, depending on what features are most important to you and how much you can afford.

The furnaces at either end of the spectrum differ markedly in how they operate. It's important to know the difference between how each functions before talking with a contractor about possibly replacing yours.

High- versus standard-efficiency furnaces

A basic fact about all forced-air furnaces is that they need to mix air with the fuel they burn to combust that fuel properly. How a furnace gets that air is one dividing line between lower- and high-efficiency furnaces. Lower-efficiency furnaces draw combustion air from the room in which they are installed; high-efficiency furnaces draw combustion air directly from outside the house. Why is this important?

Every time the burner on a standard-efficiency furnace starts up, it draws air into the combustion chamber. That air is burned along with the fuel and sent up the fluepipe.

The air comes from within the house—and therefore has been previously heated by the furnace. And as the furnace draws in air to burn, new air has to come from somewhere to replace that which is being burned up and vented outside. Additional air is drawn into the house through cracks and gaps in the exterior walls and ceiling. This creates dry conditions (exterior air is extremely dry in the winter), drafts, and inefficiency, because the incoming cold air has to be heated by the furnace.

By comparison, a super-high-efficiency, or "sealed-combustion," furnace draws its combustion air from outside the house via a PVC plastic pipe. Since the combustion air is coming directly into the firebox from outside, room air is not being burned up and vented out the flue. Because there is no demand for additional air drawn from within the house, there is no continual influx of cold, dry air from outside. The result is much greater efficiency, fewer drafts, not as many problems with dry air, and a warmer, more comfortable house.

It should be said, however, that building codes require an air-intake pipe that provides outdoor air in the vicinity of fuel-burning heating and water-heating equipment. This allows the burners to draw air from outside the house for combustion, but the intake is not as controlled as it is with sealed combustion units. And many older homes with equipment installed before the code requirement lack an air-intake pipe.

Two speeds are better than one

While 95-percent-efficiency furnaces offer homeowners the greatest benefit in terms of energy savings, lower

AFUE-rated units have also been upgraded to provide better comfort and efficiency. One feature showing up on many
sub-90-percent newer furnaces is two-stage or variable
speed burners.

Older furnaces had only one firing capacity; the burner
was either on or it was off. On a chilly—but not cold—day,
that meant the furnace might come on for only a few minutes and then shut off again, having quickly raised the
indoor temperature. Running a furnace that way is inefficient. It can be compared to starting a car to drive only a
few blocks, then shutting it off only to turn it on again to
drive a few more blocks. Cars and furnaces are both more
efficient when they can run at their optimum operating
temperatures.

Two-stage and variable-speed furnaces use sensors
to control the flow rate of the fuel through the burner. On
chilly—but not cold—days, the furnace runs at the low setting, but for a longer period of time. This allows it to operate
at the most efficient temperature and without the many
stops and starts that create inefficient burning. On cold days
it burns at full capacity to accommodate the more demanding heat load. Most two-stage and variable-speed furnaces
run at low settings approximately 90 percent of the time.

In addition to saving money, running the burner and
blower longer at low settings distributes air in rooms more
evenly and pushes more air through the furnace filter,
which results in cleaner air.

Run silent
In recent years, furnace manufacturers have been making
furnaces quieter as well as more efficient. Virtually any

newer model will be quieter than one ten years old or older. The interiors of the metal cabinets are lined with sound-absorbing material, and blower-fan blades are engineered and balanced to reduce noise.

Two-stage and variable-speed furnaces are especially quiet. A burner firing at low capacity produces less noise than one firing at full throttle, and the blower-fan speed can be reduced to integrate with the lower heat output. The combination hushes the sound of the air rushing from the heat registers.

Other furnace considerations

While furnaces have evolved over the years to offer greater comfort and efficiency, they have also become more complex. Instead of simple controls and moving parts that could be repaired or replaced by virtually anyone—even in some instances a handy homeowner—the furnaces on the market today are run by computers. And instead of a simple service call to a local furnace installer if your furnace breaks down, it requires a visit from a highly trained technician.

That simple $20 part replacement is a thing of the past, too. If a computer motherboard needs replacing in a modern furnace, the charge can run into hundreds of dollars.

The good news is that new furnaces are reliable and durable, and most offer generous warranties.

Boilers

Just about everything said about new furnaces can be applied to new gas- and oil-fired boilers. They're smaller, more efficient (some have AFUE ratings similar to those on furnaces), quieter, and more sophisticated, and some have variable-capacity burners.

High-end boilers offer sealed combustion, which eliminates the consumption of house air burned up and vented outside when the burner fires. Sensors mounted outside the house can record the temperature and adjust the boiler's water temperature to the conditions outdoors.

Features like these make boiler installation more expensive and the systems more complex but also much more energy-efficient than previous models.

So what should you do about replacing your old furnace or boiler?

Because every house and every situation is different, it is impossible to say whether or not a replacement furnace or boiler would make good economic sense for you. But if you have a large house, if you live in a cold climate, or if the price you pay for gas or oil is high, the scale tips in favor of the higher-efficiency models.

If your house is small or you live in a temperate climate, paying a premium for a super high-efficiency furnace makes less sense from a strictly economic standpoint. In that case a less expensive two-stage or variable-speed furnace or a simpler boiler might be the better value. A quality HVAC installer will take time to analyze your specific situation and can recommend the best options for your needs and budget.

Remember to consider the actual cost of heating your home—not your entire energy bill—using the simple calculation spelled out earlier in this chapter. At some point, if your heating bill is relatively low to begin with, the savings difference between an 80-percent and a 95-percent furnace doesn't amount to enough to make the larger investment worthwhile.

Also, check into whether your utility company or state energy office offers a rebate toward higher-efficiency heating and cooling equipment. Some do, and the amount tendered can sometimes pay the difference between a lower and a higher-efficiency model.

Qualified installers

Whatever you decide, if you do opt for a new furnace or boiler, be sure you are satisfied with the skill and integrity of the installer before you hire out the work. The quality of the installation matters most. Sloppy or careless work on even the best brand of HVAC equipment will result in a less-than-ideal setup that might require repeated callbacks and more time than you're willing to spend.

Be sure the installer makes a thorough energy audit of your house before you start talking about a specific furnace or boiler. One key component in how well HVAC equipment performs has to do with whether or not it is sized correctly for the anticipated heating load. Such factors as window size, number, and placement; attic and sidewall insulation; square footage of habitable space; and other items need to be accounted for in a sizing calculation. Installers use what is called a Manual J spreadsheet to arrive at the correct heat load, and from that they can recommend an ideal size furnace or boiler.

Be sure, too, if you have plans to increase the size of the house (for instance if you're going to add an addition) or its heating space (a finished basement perhaps) that the contractor knows of these impending larger demands on the heating system so it can be sized accordingly. The boiler or furnace capacity must properly fit the space it will heat. Otherwise, it will run inefficiently, might cost more than it should, and won't provide the comfort it was designed to deliver.

REPLACING THE AIR-CONDITIONING UNIT

Air-conditioning

Air-conditioning compressors are rated by their seasonal energy efficiency ratio (SEER) numbers. SEER designates the efficiency you can expect from your air-conditioning system. Higher numbers mean better efficiency. Federal regulations now mandate better energy conservation: As of 2006, only air conditioners rated 13 SEER and higher are available. If you have an older A/C compressor that you typically run a lot during the summer and you own a large house, purchasing a higher SEER unit could make economic sense.

Here's an example of how a replacement upgrade can save electrical energy and money: An older 10-SEER air conditioner requires 1,200 watts of power to produce one ton of cooling (12,000 BTUs). Every point upward results in approximately a 5 percent increase in energy efficiency. A 15-SEER rated A/C unit would consume only about 800 watts to produce that same one ton of cooling.

So, if you have a three-ton capacity A/C unit (a relatively common size), and your electrical cost is 12 cents per

What's a BTU?

Furnaces, boilers, air conditioners, kitchen ranges, and water heaters are all classified by their BTU output. But what is a "BTU"?

BTU stands for British Thermal Unit. One BTU is the amount of heat it takes to raise one pound of water one degree Fahrenheit. The burners in ranges, water heaters, boilers, and furnaces are rated by the amount of BTUs they can produce per hour.

A conventional storage-type gas water heater might have a burner rated at 35,000 or 40,000 BTUs. Forced-air gas furnaces, depending on size, might range from 25,000 up to 150,000 BTUs.

The "heat load" or cooling load on your house is calculated in BTUs, too. Wall and floor construction, wall and ceiling insulation, size of the house, number of windows, typical outdoor temperatures, and other factors are evaluated to determine how much heat or cooling—in BTUs—the house will lose per hour. Your heating and cooling equipment is sized to accommodate the BTU loss based on these calculations.

kilowatt-hour, the older 10-SEER unit will cost about 43 cents if operated continuously for an hour. (1,200 watts x 3 equals 3,600 watts. 3,600 watts divided by 1,000 equals 3.6 kilowatt-hours x 12 cents equals 43.2 cents).

Running a 15-SEER A/C of the same capacity for the same amount of time would cost 28.8 cents. (800 watts x 3 equals 2,400 watts. 2,400 watts divided by 1,000 equals 2.4 kilowatt-hours x 12 cents equals 28.8 cents.) That

14.4-cent difference for every hour of operation could add up to substantial savings over the course of a hot summer. And bear in mind that, due to deterioration and inefficient design, many A/C systems ten years old and older may be operating at only 6–9 SEER.

The highest-efficiency central A/C units on the market today are rated at about 17–18 SEER.

Run silent

Another advantage of new A/C units is that they run more quietly than previous models. This can be an important factor if you spend time outdoors around your house or if you have nearby neighbors. It's also important if you have bedrooms located close to where the outdoor compressor is situated.

Variable speed—two stage

As A/C units evolve and become more efficient, engineers devise new ways of making them work harder to achieve better comfort. One recent innovation is to equip air condi-tioners with two-stage compressors, which are somewhat similar to a two-stage furnace. On warm—but not hot—days the compressor runs using only the lower stage. This provides adequate cooling, but the compressor runs more quietly and for a longer period of time, which gives the system more of an opportunity to remove moisture from the air. The lower the humidity indoors, the higher you're likely to set the thermostat, which results in energy savings.

Variable-speed blowers alter the speed of the blower motor to most efficiently match the output of the air conditioner's compressor and condenser. This translates into better usage of the available amount of cooling, less electricity consumption, and lower energy bills.

Installation is king

Like a heating system, a cooling system has to be installed correctly and sized accurately in order to work well and maintain the efficiency for which it was designed.

For years it was common for installers to place oversize air-conditioning units in homes in order to avoid claims of insufficient cooling in the summer. This practice means an air conditioner runs for short periods of time on many days, cools the house off rapidly, and then shuts down until the thermostat calls for cooling again. The result is a home that cools quickly but doesn't run air through the evaporator coil in the furnace long enough to achieve good dehumidification—in other words, a cold but clammy house. Homeowners respond by turning down their thermostats to the point that dehumidification does take place, but at the expense of keeping the house much cooler than it needs to be.

Installers now use computer software to incorporate such information as window size and placement, insulation found in attics and sidewalls, square footage, orientation and geographical location of the house, and other factors into their sizing calculations. This enables them to precisely determine which air conditioner suits a particular house. In addition, two-stage and variable-speed A/C systems are capable of adapting themselves to provide just the right amount of cooling and dehumidifying needed for virtually any situation.

THE PLUMBING FACTOR

Consider the plumbing of your home

Do you know that 20 percent of a typical household energy bill goes toward heating water? You should keep that in mind in your quest to conserve energy and curb spending.

A tankless job

Visitors to Europe and other overseas locales are often confronted in their hotel rooms by wall-hanging tanks that their hosts inform them are instant water heaters. The tanks contain a burner or electrical heating element that heats water flowing through the unit. Open a hot-water tap, and the burner or heating element comes on; shut the tap, and the burner or element shuts off, and water heating ceases.

Tankless water heaters are energy-efficient in large part because they have virtually none of the "standby" heat loss that is inherent in the standard tank- or "storage-"type water heaters in this country. During the hours between uses, heat from a 40- or 50-gallon conventional water heater tank is eventually transferred to the surrounding air, and the burner or heating element activates in order to keep the volume of water in the tank hot. The standby heat loss also contributes to the cooling load of an air-conditioning system during the summer.

Another advantage to using a tankless water heater, though it has nothing to do with energy savings or efficiency, is that you never run out of hot water. You can take one shower or bath after another, and you never have to wait for water in a tank to heat up sufficiently to make it tolerable.

Newer models of tankless heaters contain variable-capacity burners that automatically adjust their firing to the volume and temperature of the water passing through the heat exchanger, resulting in more efficient heating and more precise output temperature. Ignition is supplied by a sparking device, eliminating energy loss due to a standing pilot light. Tankless water heater burners are also more efficient than storage water heater burners.

Manufacturers continue to refine the mechanics on tankless water heaters. They are now available for purchase at plumbing supply houses, lumberyards, and home centers in the United States.

What size?

Installing a tankless water heater in a home is more complicated than one might think. You can't simply replace a standard tank-type water heater with a tankless model. A key issue is sizing the new unit correctly. Tankless water heaters are rated by their ability to raise the temperature of the water coming into the unit at a certain flow rate. One complaint some have about these devices is that if they aren't sized properly, they aren't capable of delivering enough water to serve several uses at the same time. Both of these problems are usually due to the unit being undersized for the anticipated usage. Another complaint is that when multiple people in a house attempt to use the hot water simultaneously, nobody gets enough of it.

Baby, it's cold outside

Say you live in Michigan, it's winter, and the water coming
into your home is a frigid 38 degrees. It takes a lot of
energy to heat that water to a usable 120 degrees or so.
To ensure the water is being heated to the correct temperature, a tankless water heater might have to slow the
flow rate through the heat exchanger. This can result in
a lower-than-expected volume of water at the hot-water
tap or shower.

Or, given the same geographical and climatic situation, if
two people in the house want to use hot water at the same
time, those two users might have to share the hot water
coming out of the water heater—and neither is likely to be
satisfied with how much they are getting.

The key to avoiding these problems is to purchase a
tankless water heater with enough capacity to deal with any
circumstance—or to accept and work around some of the
limitations of a smaller model.

Other tankless implications

A quirk about tankless water heaters is that they require
a certain flow rate through the unit in order to activate the
switch that turns on the burner. Unless you're using a half
gallon of water per minute, the burner won't fire, and you
won't get any hot water. Tankless heaters also require
5-15 seconds to heat water to its desired temperature. In
large homes where there are already long waits for hot
water, the additional time it takes to reach the user may
seem interminable, and it also wastes water.

On the plus side, many tankless water heaters are only
about the size of a large suitcase, and they are designed to
hang on a wall. This can free up valuable floor space.

Installation issues

If you decide to look further into installing a tankless water heater, be aware that you will likely have to deal with some gas piping, fluepipe, and electrical issues. The gas units (which have the highest capacity, and thus are the most popular type) require a flue to vent combustion by-products created by the burner's firing. Because burners on tankless water heaters require a high volume of gas, they require a larger-than-normal flue to safely vent the combustion gases. So you usually can't simply replace a standard tank-type water heater with a tankless one and expect to hook up the flue to the chimney where the old water-heater flue used to go.

New models of tankless water heaters, like sealed combustion furnaces, can vent out a sidewall through a plastic PVC pipe, thus eliminating the need to upsize an existing fluepipe. However, if an old tank-type water heater shares its flue with the furnace, removing that old flue pipe in order to install a sidewall-vented tankless water heater could mean that the furnace flue will have to be downsized to safely handle the furnace-only flue gases. It gets complicated, and that's why installing a tankless water heater, while beneficial from an energy-efficiency standpoint in most cases, needs to be thought through carefully, and it is probably not an ideal do-it-yourself project.

Because of a tankless water heater's outsized burner capacity, gas piping might have to be replaced with a larger size in order to deliver the amount of gas necessary for the water heater to operate correctly. And most tankless water heaters require electricity to operate, meaning a new receptacle might have to be added if one is not already within six feet of the planned installation. Dependence on electricity, of course, means the water heater won't heat water during power outages, though some of the newest models on the market are designed to operate without outside power. The heat exchanger inside a tankless water heater requires periodic descaling in hard-water areas, using a mild acid liquid, but the service life of the unit should be 20 years or more.

Finally, the initial cost of a tankless water heater is usually several times that of a storage-type water heater. Additional money is often required for installation expenses. But if you use a lot of hot water and can live with some of a tankless water heater's quirks, then investing in one can result in energy savings over its lifetime.

NEW APPLIANCES

Energy Star

In 1992, the federal government developed an energy-efficiency rating program called "Energy Star." Energy Star is now jointly administered by the Environmental Protection Agency (EPA) and the Department of Energy (DOE). The Energy Star Web site at www.energystar.gov provides appliance ratings and tips on improving the energy performance of your home and business.

The appliance-labeling program, perhaps the most visible of Energy Star's endeavors, rates major appliances and provides information that allows consumers to make energy-wise choices about these products.

How much can new appliances save?

Energy Star-qualified appliances exceed federal energy-efficiency standards by 10 to 50 percent. As an example, Energy Star-rated refrigerators use better-quality insulation, more efficient compressors, and more sophisticated temperature-control mechanisms, delivering 15 percent better energy savings than other models that only meet the current government standards.

Because a refrigerator typically uses the most energy of any appliance in a household, these energy improvements can make a noticeable difference in energy and money saved. Energy Star-rated freezers use the same improvements to yield at least a 10-percent premium on energy savings.

Similar numbers show up in ratings for dishwashers, clothes washers, dehumidifiers, ceiling fans, and HVAC

Should a Ceiling Fan Blow Down or Up?

There is a switch on the side of most ceiling fans that controls the direction of the blade rotation. In the summer it's best if the blades blow air downward onto the occupants of the room. That provides a cooling, wind-chill effect as air blows over the skin.

The downward push of air, however, can make the room feel drafty and cooler than it really is in the winter. Thus that's the time of year to switch the blade rotation so the fan pulls air upward. That moves stratified warm air off the ceiling and down along the walls, creating a more even mix of air in the room.

equipment. And while Energy Star-rated appliances and electronic devices usually bear a higher price tag than models without the Energy Star rating, the extra cost is more than made up in savings over the lifetime of the product.

Energy Star-rated appliances like dishwashers and clothes washers make the most sense in homes where these are frequently used. Larger homes, or ones that are located in severe climate areas like the north or the south, can save by using Energy Star-rated heating and cooling equipment.

And here's an energy-saving tip that is appropriate anywhere: If you have an older refrigerator or freezer in your garage or basement for beverages, get rid of it. You might be spending up to 25 dollars a month just to keep such an antiquated energy hog going. Plus, a hot garage environment makes the inefficient compressor work even harder to achieve cooling.

Washing machines

Front-loading clothes-washing machines are considered the standard in Europe and also in commercial applications in this country. Expensive energy sources and smaller living spaces drive the overseas use of these machines, and now they're starting to replace top-loading washing machines in this country.

The advantages of front loaders in terms of energy savings alone are compelling, but they have other features that recommend them as well. Front-loading machines use only one third to one half of the water that conventional top loaders do. Because some wash water needs to be heated, reducing the volume used means the water heater doesn't have to produce as much, resulting in energy savings—with water savings as a bonus.

Some new clothes washers include a heating element that can be activated much like the one in a dishwasher to heat water in the machine higher than the temperature the household water heater produces. This feature can be used for special purposes, for instance to sanitize baby wear or to wash sheets and pillowcases during cold and flu season.

Front-loading washing machines clean clothes by dropping them through and dipping them into water repeatedly during the wash cycle instead of swishing them back and forth, as is the norm in top-loading washers. The drum spins on a horizontal axis rather than a vertical one. Tests indicate that this type of washing action cleans clothes better and more gently. Front loaders also use high-speed rinse and water-extraction cycles—some can spin the drum at 1,400 rpm, which yields more thorough removal of water and soap residue.

Because higher spin speeds remove more water, clothing needs less time to finish drying, which yields savings. Shortened drying times also mean clothing items have less contact with each other in the high-heat environment, helping the fabric last longer.

Front-loading washing machines and matching dryers can be stacked atop one another, saving valuable floor space. This means that the laundry pair might be able to fit into an area where a conventional side-by-side setup couldn't go. And many people find it is easier to load and remove clothes from a front-loading machine.

Another advantage of front-loading washing machines is that, because they use less water, they require less soap and bleach to clean clothes. However, many front loaders require the use of special low-sudsing detergents in order to work properly.

Top loaders

To keep pace with the interest in water and energy-saving front loaders, manufacturers of top-loading machines now offer models with competing features. Some new machines on the market have no central agitator. Others offer high-speed water-extraction spin cycles. Most use less water than previous designs and consequently require less soap and bleach. However, some do need low-suds detergent to operate optimally.

A trip to an appliance store or a visit to a manufacturer's Web site can help you sort through all the offerings and decide what type of washing machine best fits your individual needs.

Dryers

The Energy Star program doesn't rate dryers because they all use similar amounts of energy. Nevertheless, a good way to control the energy used to dry clothing is to turn on the automatic-drying feature on the dryer if it has one instead of a timer. This useful feature employs a sensor that measures the amount of moisture in the air exiting the dryer. Once the moisture level in that air is reduced to a certain level, the dryer shuts off. No more fuel or electricity is used than is necessary to dry a load of clothes.

The timed dryer cycle, on the other hand, will keep heating and tumbling a load of clothes even after they are dry, until the set time is finished. Not only does this waste fuel and electricity, it also unnecessarily heats and wears down the clothes, shortening their life.

Dishwashers

If you're thinking of purchasing a new dishwasher, carefully consider your needs before making a final decision. These appliances come in standard and compact sizes. If you live in a home where a lot of cooking takes place and a lot of dirty dishes are generated, the standard size is the more practical choice. Because hot water use constitutes the largest expense connected with operating a dishwasher, running it with full loads is a smart idea. If you have to load and run a compact dishwasher several times in order to clean up after a meal, it costs more in terms of hot-water usage and electricity compared to operating a larger machine one time.

Dishwashers are built with heating elements inside that boost the temperature of the water to at least 140 degrees, which sterilizes dishes. This heat boost is also necessary to allow detergent to dissolve properly and to clean as it was formulated to do. Owning a dishwasher with a water heating element means you don't have to keep the household water heater at 140 degrees to accommodate the dishwasher's needs; a practice which is both a scalding hazard and a waste of energy.

WHAT ABOUT WINDOWS?

Windows—a new outlook

The marketplace is inundated these days with window choices. A component that was once an afterthought when a new home was being built, windows now command multiple advertising pages in builders and home improvement magazines. Windows, both for new construction and for replacement, are big business. What constitutes a good window?

Virtually any new window you purchase will have at least two panes of glass making up the glazing. Only those designed for use in unheated areas like garages are likely to have a single pane of glass.

Two-pane, or insulated, glass has proven its worth over the decades. Sandwiching air between two separated, sealed panes increases the insulative value of the glazing many times. In recent years manufacturers have even upped the ante by sealing gases like argon and krypton, which have more density and better insulative qualities than plain air, inside that space.

The glass in the assembly can also be coated with nearly invisible films, like Low-e metallic oxides, that can be manipulated to impart various properties to the window, like better heat retention or solar heat reduction.

The sash that holds the glazing is also important to the overall thermal performance of the window. Materials that offer low heat conductance, like wood, hollow or insulation-filled vinyl, or fiberglass help reduce the transference of cold inside and heat outside.

All these improvements make both replacement and original windows more energy-efficient than they've ever been. And the technology has also increased the comfort factor. Sitting next to a single-pane window in the winter can make you feel cold, even when the house itself is sufficiently warm. Heat from your body is radiated out the window. But energy-efficient glazing keeps the inside pane of glass warmer. That reflects your body heat back inside, making you feel more comfortable and saving energy.

From an energy-efficiency standpoint, one of the most important improvements to modern windows is the increase in the performance of weather stripping that stops air from infiltrating. Anyone who has lived (or is presently living) in a house that has leaky windows knows how the wind outside can rustle draperies inside. That leakiness adds up to wasted energy. New windows, if properly installed, won't leak air and will save energy as a result.

Window ratings

The nonprofit National Fenestration Rating Council rates some manufacturers' windows based on air leakage, U-factor (a gauge that represents the window's rate of heat loss), visual transmittance (a measure of the amount of light the window lets into a room), and the solar-heat-gain coefficient (a measure of the solar heat gain possible through that window).

Labels on windows rated by the Council tell you what to expect from the manufacturers' products, and this information allows you to select different windows to satisfy different criteria for each area of your house. For instance, good properties to have in a southerly facing window in a house located in the northern part of the country would be a good solar-heat-gain coefficient rating, low air leakage, and an excellent U-factor. For a window in the same house facing in a northerly direction, the solar-heat-gain coefficient wouldn't be worth paying for, while the U-factor and air leakage rating would be even more important.

Install it right

Even good windows will not live up to their billing if they are installed improperly. That's why selecting an experienced,

Time It Right

If you're thinking of doing an energy efficiency upgrade on your house, where should you start? Air sealing is usually the first priority. Sealing as many of the gaps and holes as you can get to in the attic ceiling and on the home's exterior reduces the amount of air that escapes the house and leaks into the attic.

After the air sealing is complete, attic insulation can be blown or laid on top of the air-sealed attic floor.

If you're going to have windows replaced and a new heating or air-conditioning unit installed, consider getting the windows replaced first. When a contractor sizes the equipment for the expected heating and cooling load of the house, the contractor will take into consideration the energy upgrades you've done first. If there are new windows in place and thick insulation in the attic, plus a good amount of air sealing replaced, the result is that cooling and heating loads will be reduced. Therefore, you might be able to get by with a smaller (and less expensive) heating or cooling unit.

conscientious installer is important to maximize both the energy efficiency and your satisfaction with the windows you purchase.

Window installation is complex. Any part of the job that is left to chance can come back to haunt the homeowner with water leaks, dysfunctional opening and closing, poor energy performance, and air leakage—everything you paid good money to avoid. This is particularly true when it comes to replacement windows, where old materials have to be incorporated into the new installation.

An improvement over the old windows

Virtually any new window installed in an older home will improve energy efficiency. This is especially true if the old windows are in poor condition. How much could you save in utility bills? That's hard to predict. It depends on how leaky the old windows are, the quality of the windows with which you're replacing them, and the quality of the installation. But beyond the energy savings, one of the most important improvements you will likely notice right away is the way upgraded windows make a house feel cozier, quieter, warmer, and more secure.

Installing new windows in an existing home makes the house "live larger." In other words, if your old windows were so leaky that the cold made you stay away from them in the winter, you confined yourself to a smaller area of the house. If reading at night by a window made you feel cold, you retreated farther toward the middle of the house in order to stay warm. The same might be true if you upgrade your windows to block out sun or heat in southern climates. It's uncomfortable sitting in the sunlight inside if the house already feels too warm. New windows might allow you to sit near the exterior walls of the house in greater comfort, in effect increasing its square footage.

New windows can also affect your attitude about your house and neighborhood. Along with stopping air leakage, modern windows are much more effective at blocking noise. Traffic, air conditioners running in the summer, and other normal neighborhood noise might not be as distracting with new windows.

Homeowners who are either tired of or not capable of climbing ladders to clean windows outside the house will appreciate the tilt-in sash feature on most new windows. With just a flick of two buttons you have access to the exterior glass for cleaning. This saves time and is much safer than climbing a ladder to do the job.

Old windows—are they worth keeping?

Despite all the advantages of new windows, economic or historical concerns may be a factor in considering window upgrading. While it is true that no original single-pane glass window can match the thermal performance of a new window, it's surprising how close it can come—albeit with a lot of work.

If you own a house with historical features, it is worth considering restoring rather than replacing your original windows. There are situations when even the best new windows look out of place, and one of those is in a house that was designed and built with architecturally significant windows. While not impossible to duplicate today, such windows can be prohibitively expensive to reproduce. The solution is to make the existing windows as energy-efficient as possible.

Old windows usually require at least scraping and painting, and perhaps glazing compound replacement. You'll also need to repair broken sash cords or chains just to get them working properly and safely again. If they are in poor condition, some might require the re-gluing of joints, epoxy or wood repairs to the sash, total glass removal and re-glazing, and maybe even some replacement of cracked or broken panes.

From there, you can upgrade thermal performance by adding weather stripping around the perimeter of the window sash and along the meeting rail between double-hung windows. You can also install draft-blocking devices that plug the cord or chain holes and reduce the amount of air infiltration from those portals. To achieve the best efficiency possible, adding storm windows to either the outside of the house or to the interior will help thermal performance considerably.

If every advantage is taken, if all weather stripping is installed properly, and if storm windows are added to the outside, it is possible to achieve near-new window performance with old windows. However, while the outlay for materials to restore older windows is relatively low, the labor factor is high. This is a good job for those handy enough to do the repairs or for those with the means to hire professionals.

Older windows can last for 100 years or more if maintained attentively. Modern windows are unlikely to hold up that long.

CONSIDER WHOLE HOUSE ISSUES

When you work on your home to make it more energy efficient and less expensive to maintain, you must also consider safety issues.

- **When weatherizing, be certain you have sufficient "additional" air for your furnace, water heater, and clothes dryer.**

- **Create proper ventilation in the attic to prevent ice dams on the roof in the winter and unwanted heat in the summer.**

- **Do your homework before you hire a contractor: Look for both reasonable prices and quality labor.**

ADEQUATE VENTILATION

Too tight?

Houses are made up of many different components that work together as a system. If you change one part of that system, the other parts are affected. As you make your

home more airtight and energy efficient, you also alter the
way it functions.

A previously unweatherized house typically has a leaky
shell. Air from outside is free to infiltrate and exfiltrate
through various uncaulked and unfilled cracks, gaps, and
holes in the exterior. When you stop up those leaks, replace
old windows, caulk, and fill, thus removing some of the
pathways through which air formerly entered the house.

From the standpoint of saving energy this is a good thing.
The less air that leaves the house, the less heating and
cooling need to be produced in order to replace it. But is
there such a thing as a house that is too airtight?

The answer is that it really isn't possible to make a
house too airtight. It is possible, however, to make it too
poorly ventilated. Where is the dividing line?

Potential hazards of weatherizing a house

Systems in the house require a reliable influx of air to operate properly. Specifically, these are the items that burn fuel
on site and then exhaust combustion by-products outside
through a vent or fluepipe, such as furnaces, boilers, water
heaters, fireplaces, and gas clothes dryers. If a house is
made relatively airtight AND not enough combustion air is
provided for these fuel-burners, problems can result.

Here's an example: A furnace or boiler burns fuel in
order to heat a house. The fuel (either gas or oil) requires
mixing with air in order to combust properly. When the
burner on a conventional furnace or boiler fires up, it draws
air into a combustion chamber. The air mixes with the fuel,
the mixture is burned up, and the exhaust gases are vented
outside. Air rushing into the combustion chamber and then

up the fluepipe has to come from somewhere. This air has to be replaced, or made up.

In poorly weatherized houses, this "make-up air" can enter through the variety of gaps in the building's exterior shell. Since it's easy for the air to enter this way, such gaps are referred to as "paths of least resistance." But what happens when you start to close these pathways? Where does make-up air come from then?

If you tighten up your home's exterior and do not make provisions to provide the fuel-burning equipment on site

---

Going Away?

If you leave home for more than a couple of days, you can reduce your utility bill—and also protect your house—by doing simple things before you walk out the door.

First, unplug any appliances that don't need to be on while you're away, including the TV, VCR, DVD player, cable box, computers and their peripherals, stereo systems, and microwave oven. All of these devices use electricity even when they're off, and they also can be harmed by power surges. Plus, electrical items can short-circuit and cause fires (though rarely).

Second, if you have a gas water heater, turn the thermostat dial to the "Vacation" setting. That setting still keeps the pilot light lit, but the burner won't fire in order to keep the tank full of hot water. Mark the dial before you turn it down so you'll be able to quickly dial it back up to its former setting when you return. If you have an electric water heater, flip the disconnect or breaker to shut off its power.

with a source of make-up air, the air may be drawn down different—and less desirable—pathways. One of these might be the water heater's fluepipe.

For example, a problem might arise when a water heater and furnace happen to operate at the same time. Both demand make-up air. If not enough air is freely available, the furnace can draw make-up air from the water heater's fluepipe. Should this occur, combustion by-products produced by the water heater are vented back down the fluepipe and into the house. This condition is

Third, shut off the water to the house at the main shut-off valve and open a faucet or two in order to relieve pressure in the pipes. The hoses on clothes washers burst with surprising regularity, and if this happens when you're away from the house, the basement could fill up with water. In addition, the house will be protected in the winter should a power failure occur when it is cold enough inside the house to freeze water in the pipes.

Fourth, turn your thermostat down as far as it will go in the winter—most can drop to 55 degrees. In the summer, just turn the thermostat to "off." Why heat or cool a house when no one is around to benefit?

Fifth, put a couple of lights on timers, set to run an hour or two at night in order to make the house look occupied.

Sixth, make friends with your neighbors so they can look in on your place every day or so. There's no substitute for a set of eyes watching over your house while you're away.

called "backdrafting," and it has potentially dangerous consequences.

Combustion by-products, such as those produced by fuel-burning water heaters, boilers, furnaces, fireplaces, and gas clothes dryers, contain carbon monoxide gas, a poison that is taken up by the body's red blood cells in place of oxygen. According to the Consumer Product Safety Commission (CPSC), approximately 125 people in the United States die every year of carbon-monoxide poisoning. Some of those deaths are attributed to backdrafting conditions from fuel-burning devices.

Backdrafting can also occur when exterior-vented fan devices operate. A kitchen range hood is a good example, as well as bathroom ventilation fans. Anything that pushes air out of the house reduces the air pressure inside, and make-up air has to come from somewhere in order to replace the air that is lost. The more airtight the house, the greater the potential for backdrafting.

The solution to backdrafting is to provide enough make-up air for fuel-burning equipment to operate correctly. Building codes require a make-up air inlet to be piped into the mechanical room in all new homes. Older homes, however, often lack such a pipe.

Therefore, you should consult your furnace or boiler service person before you do any tightening of your home's shell. It could be that your house already has a make-up-air pipe in place. If it doesn't, one can be easily added.

One more note about fuel-burning items in the home. If you opt to have a furnace or boiler replaced with a new, energy-efficient model, consider paying more for a high-efficiency sealed combustion unit. These systems draw combustion air directly from outside the house. This eliminates the need for a lot of make-up air, though you still might need some for a gas- or oil-fired water heater.

Carbon monoxide detectors

To alert you to the possibility that backdrafting or another problem is occurring, every house should have carbon-monoxide (CO) detectors installed. Smoke detectors are required in all homes, but in many parts of the country CO detectors are not. Costing as little as $40 or so, CO detectors can alert you to a potentially dangerous buildup of the colorless, odorless, and tasteless gas.

As described earlier, carbon monoxide found in the house environment can result from improperly burning and venting fuel-burning heating equipment like furnaces, boilers, space heaters, and fireplaces. It can also come from gas or oil water heaters, gas ranges, clothes dryers, and even from automobile exhaust that leaks or is drawn into the house from an attached garage.

The usual recommendation is that a CO detector be placed in or near the sleeping quarters in a house. That way even if you're asleep, the alarm will alert you when the detector picks up the presence of the gas in the house. It is a good idea to place a second detector in or near the mechanical room. Venting malfunction is most likely to occur in this area.

Municipal fire departments often have programs that give smoke detectors away for free. Some are starting to do the same with CO detectors.

Other airtightness issues

Many people observe that after they have some types of energy upgrading done in their homes, conditions inside change markedly, especially during the winter. One common scenario is that after a homeowner has her or his old windows replaced with new ones, she or he will start noticing excess moisture inside the house—notably condensation on cold mornings on the inside panes of the new window glass. What happened?

Old windows are usually not very airtight. They allow air to infiltrate the house and also to leave the house. This sets up an uncontrolled ventilation pattern that removes moisture from inside the house (in the form of water vapor) and imports dry air from outside. The result is dry air inside during most of the winter—a common complaint from those who live in leaky older homes.

Once the old, leaky windows are replaced with airtight new ones, that indoor moisture no longer has a means of escape. It builds up to levels that can create condensation on cold surfaces. Since window glazing is usually the coldest surface in most houses, that's where the condensation shows up first. This is one of the most common complaints to window companies. Customers who thought having new windows installed would rid them of condensation on their windows sometimes find just the opposite to be the case: They're getting more condensation than ever.

The new windows are not at fault. There is simply too much humidity in the house. The solution is to reduce the humidity level inside. After that the condensation is reduced or disappears.

Homeowners who undertake comprehensive air sealing in their homes often find similar problems with moisture

Shades of Energy Savings

Adding or upgrading window shades can cut heat and cooling losses significantly. In addition, they provide privacy, solar heat and light control, and a reduction of sound transmission from outside the house.

Simple vinyl, wood, or metal slatted window blinds don't add much insulative value. Generally speaking, the heavier and more solid the shade the better the energy conservation qualities. Roman-type shades that drop down from a top-mounting bar are an example of a solid shade through which heat and cooling can migrate.

Lining any type of shade increases its thickness and insulative effectiveness. "Cellular" or "honeycomb" shades unfold to create air pockets between layers of the material, and some even pack the "cells" with cotton batt-type insulation.

Sealing the sides and bottom of the shade to the window trim and sill makes the installation even more effective. Some shade systems come with magnetic strips that mount on the trim and have corresponding metal material sewn into the shade. As the shades come down or unfold, the strip and trim form a relatively airtight seal.

buildup. They've cut off the ventilation that diluted the humidity and brought in drier air from outside.

Similarly, an upgrade to sealed combustion furnaces and boilers can lead to issues with excess humidity. The problem lies in the fact that drier outdoor air that used to be drawn into the house by the combustion process in the old furnace is no longer streaming inside. That means the air inside the house is not being replaced with outdoor air. Humid air that was formerly diluted with the incoming drier air is now predominant and condensation difficulties can crop up.

Air quality

In the absence of sufficient air exchange with the outdoors, indoor air can start to suffer quality problems. Odors from cooking and pets, off-gassing from building materials and furnishings, radon gas, combustion by-products from gas ranges, and other pollutants can accumulate. Studies reveal that, because we spend approximately 90 percent of our time indoors, exposure to these items can be dangerous—especially for children, seniors, and those who suffer from cardiovascular or respiratory diseases. The solution is to increase ventilation in order to dilute and exhaust the problem air.

Source control

One good way to reduce humidity and air pollutants is to attack the problem of poor indoor air quality at the source. Because bathroom fans reduce the level of indoor humidity by venting water vapor to the outside, be sure to turn on the fan when you bathe or shower. Also, turn on the fan to a kitchen range hood while cooking to vent odors and humidity. This is especially important when you use a gas range or oven. Gas ranges produce combustion by-products that collect in the house unless vented. Some range hoods, however, remove only gaseous pollutants like combustion by-products when they vent to the outside, and many range hoods do not even do that. Recirculating-type range hoods are somewhat effective at removing airborne grease, but they do not take combustion by-products out of the air.

Whole house solutions

Air filters, either stand-alone or furnace-mounted, can be helpful in straining dust and dead skin cells (from both humans and pets) from the air, but they are not effective at removing gas-type pollutants.

One of the best methods of reducing the level and impact of indoor air pollutants and excess humidity is to mix the indoor air with fresh, dry air from outside the house. But after you've just spent hours and dollars trying to increase the airtightness of your house in order to make it more energy-efficient, how do you increase the ventilation without reducing the effect of everything you've accomplished?

First of all, it's hard to make an older home so airtight that indoor air pollution becomes a major problem—or at least one that can't be solved by taking one or two simple steps to alleviate the condition. Old houses just have too many places where air can leak out (and outdoor air can be drawn in). You'll never be able to find and plug them all. Newer homes are generally more airtight from the start.

If your house feels stale, stuffy, or excessively humid, simply opening a door or window for a few minutes each day will replace some of the bad air with good air.

Homeowners with children may find that this procedure takes place naturally, as incoming and outgoing traffic continually pumps air in and out of the house. If you need to resort to occasionally ventilating by opening doors and windows, the heat loss will be minimal if you don't leave them open for too long.

For homes with chronic indoor air quality problems that can't be eliminated or reduced by manual ventilation and removing the pollutants and humidity at the source, other means are available to introduce fresh air to your home with minimal heat loss. Heat recovery ventilators (HRVs) use fans to continually bring air in from outside the house. As incoming air enters the HRV, it passes through a heat exchanger that is kept warm by the indoor air exiting the other side. Because the two air streams never mix, the only thing transferred from the outgoing air stream to the incoming one is heat. And while there is not a 100-percent heat transfer, the exchange is efficient enough that the incoming fresh air can be quickly warmed by the home's heating system.

An HRV can be installed either as a stand-alone system or tied into forced-air furnace ducting. The fans, used to pull in and push out the air, are small, but they do use some electricity. Filters can be added to the installation in order to clean the incoming air before it enters the house. An HRV installed correctly should be virtually unnoticeable to the homeowner. There should be little or no noise and the mix of incoming air with the air already inside the house should not create drafts or cold spots. An HRV can also be shut off when it is not needed.

Energy efficiency and ice dams

If you have ice dams forming on your roof during the winter, it means that heat is escaping the house and leaking into your attic. Ice dams are the manifestation of energy inefficiency in a home. They are the result of poor air sealing, a lack of insulation, and inadequate ventilation in an attic.

Warm air travels upward because of its natural buoyancy. As it reaches the ceiling in the top floor, it seeks ways to rise even higher through cracks and gaps in the ceiling and walls. Some of those pathways are obvious; many others are not. As discussed in earlier chapters, openings around and through recessed canister lights, whole-house fan installations, attic-access hatchways and pull-down stairs, and electrical boxes in the ceiling and walls all provide conduits from the house into the attic. Additionally, heat is conducted upward through the top-floor ceiling through inadequate attic floor insulation. The result of the air leaks and conducted heat is an accumulation of warm air in the attic.

When snow falls on top of a roof, it acts as insulation, protecting the roof surface from the outside cold air. The combination of heat from below and snow on top creates conditions that warm the roof sheathing and shingles.

The warm shingles melt the snow that covers them, and that water runs down the roof, under the snowpack that lies on top of the roof. As the water reaches the roof edge, there is no longer any heat from below to warm the shingles and sustain the melting process. The water freezes along the overhangs and starts to build into ice dams.

As the ice dams build up higher over the course of the winter due to the constantly melting snow on the roof, water starts to form ponds behind the dams. Eventually, if the water level gets high enough and if the roof is inadequately protected from water intrusion, it starts to seep in underneath the shingles. In the worst cases the water can penetrate into the soffit areas, get behind the siding, and even enter the house through the interior ceilings and walls. Ice dams can be very destructive and result in millions of dollars in insurance claims every year.

The root cause of ice dams is excess heat in the attic. Undertaking the air sealing and insulating measures described earlier in this book will help reduce the heat leakage problem. The idea is to make the attic as cold as possible—as cold as the outside air—to reduce or eliminate the snow melting that starts the ice dam formation process. Additional ventilation in the attic also exhausts any heat that does manage to make it up there.

The ideal ventilation scheme involves several components: soffit vents that introduce air into the attic under the eave edges; air channels; chutes that hold insulation back from the underside of the roof sheathing and direct the air upward from the soffits into the attic; and high roof or ridge vents that convey the air to the outdoors. The chutes are important because insulation lying against the underside of the roof sheathing forms a thermal bridge that allows heat from the house below to travel through the insulation directly to the sheathing. It is essential to break that thermal bridge to eliminate the direct conveyance of the heat to the sheathing and to promote the free flow of air into the rest of the attic from the soffit vents.

Attic ventilation is also needed to reduce moisture concentration in the attic environment. Air that travels into the attic from the house below carries water vapor. Unless that moisture is vented away, it can condense on the cold insulation, framing, and sheathing. If allowed to continue, the wet surroundings can create conditions conducive to mildew and mold growth, and can even rot.

Adequate attic ventilation also pays off in the summer. Air flowing through the soffit vents and up through the ridge or high roof vents exhausts heat. Venting the attic means less heat is transferred downward through the attic floor insulation and into the house below. Therefore, the A/C doesn't have to run as often, which conserves your energy dollars.

Comprehensive air sealing, insulation, and ventilation can reduce or eliminate the formation of ice dams on your house roof in the winter while paying dividends in the summer. Plus, this type of energy-saving upgrading is a one-time event in the life of the house. Add vents and insulation and perform air sealing, and you'll never have to worry about it again.

KNOW YOUR CONTRACTORS

Talking to contractors about working on your house

Any type of contact with a professional you hire to do work in your home is likely to create stress. You are concerned about getting the best value for your money, you don't know whom to call first or whom to hire to do a certain type of work, and you're nervous about opening up your home to someone who is likely a complete stranger. Also at risk is the integrity of the house itself. If you hire someone who does the work incompetently, what are the consequences?

At stake are money, time, and your sense of security in your own home.

It is generally recommended that you get at least three estimates from contractors to do any type of work on your home. In some areas that is a tough mission to accomplish. Either there aren't many contractors around who do the particular type of work you want done, or if there are, you may have a difficult time deciding exactly whom to call from a long list. Consequently, many homeowners ask around at their workplaces, churches, schools, or at social gatherings for the names of contractors who have done similar work for their neighbors, friends, or colleagues.

Recommendations from others are often successful because you can ask them about the manner in which the contractor conducted himself or herself while on the job. Was the contractor on time for appointments? Did the project come in on budget—and, equally important—on time? Were the workers respectful and did they clean up after themselves? Did the quality of the job meet your expectations? But keep in mind: A contractor who did satisfactory work for one client might not perform as well for another, and the perception of that contractor might also vary from client to client.

Hiring out contracting work is in many ways risky. You don't know exactly what you're getting until the job is complete. The scope and timing of the job can change along the way; you might have personality conflicts with the people hired to do the work; the workers might find something that was not anticipated in the job that costs more money to remedy. Really, anything can happen between signing the initial contact and the final billing.

But you can increase the odds of a successful encounter with someone you hire if you do a little homework first.

Your initial task is to find out from your local building department or state building regulation office what licenses and qualifications are necessary for a contractor to do the type of work you want done in your home. Also ask about insurance requirements. It comes as a surprise to many homeowners to learn that if a worker is injured on a job site and is not covered under a contractor's Worker's Compensation policy, the homeowner—or the homeowner's insurance—is responsible for the injured party. Be sure any contractor you hire has the proper regulatory qualifications, licenses, and insurance in place before you consider him for the job. Because contractors are used to being asked for documentary paperwork, those who have their bases covered with respect to these questions will have the necessary documents on hand.

After you've narrowed the search down to three or four candidates, try to meet with each to determine if you'll be able to work well together. Long projects or disruptive ones require very close contact between the homeowner and contractor. There are other contractors around with whom you might be able to forge a working relationship.

If you're comfortable with a contractor, be sure any estimates for the work you want done are written down, along with a comprehensive summary of the scope of the work, material specifications, and a timetable. Some homeowners request clauses in a contract that penalize the contractor for each day the job is unfinished after a set date—though these are usually reserved for larger projects that might take months to complete. Be sure each party understands the part he or she will play in the work process. Communication between a contractor and a homeowner is vital for work to proceed smoothly toward a successful conclusion.

There should be a payment schedule included in the final contract. It is not unusual for a contractor to ask for a portion of the money up front in order to get started on the job. Such payments are negotiable, though the contractor might have a set percentage that he or she always works with. Be sure the contract reserves your right to withhold final payment until you are satisfied that the job has been completed as specified.

Hiring someone to work on your home might seem daunting at first. But the more time and effort you put into it—and the better prepared you are with information you obtained up front and by asking pertinent questions—the better your project will turn out. Millions of homeowners hire contractors to do work on their homes each year, and the majority of those jobs turn out satisfactorily for both parties. The ones that do not, however, often make headlines—much to the detriment of the bulk of honest, hardworking, and knowledgeable contractors.

ALTERNATIVE ENERGY SOURCES

There is a growing movement in this country toward the exploration of sources of alternative energy—solar heating, electrical generation, wind power, and hydro power. While a comprehensive discussion of those matters is beyond the scope of this book, for homeowners who live in areas that have conditions suitable for alternative power generation, one or more of those sources could be valuable in reducing dependence on fossil fuels on both an individual and a national basis.

Electricity blowing in the wind

Large wind-powered generators are being built in many places throughout the country. Wind energy is also a potential source of power for individual homeowners. In order to produce electricity with a wind generator, however, there has to be a reliable source of wind to turn the blades of a turbine. You also need either storage for the power generated on site or a means to tap into the power grid. Connection to the grid ensures that that you can use some of the utility company's power when your wind generator is not producing. When the generator is producing excess power, it can be sold to the utility company. Investment in an individual wind turbine is expensive, even more so for onsite power storage with sufficient capacity to power an entire house.

Running water

Individual hydro applications are very demanding in their site specifications, requiring a steady source of running water that falls a certain distance. The places where individual hydro power generation can work are few and far between, but in the right location the power is reliable and consistent.

Harnessing the sun

Solar water and space heating, as well as electrical power generation, offer perhaps the most widespread applications. Many individual solar water heating systems are already in place in this country, and they provide free hot water either year-round or just during the sunnier months, depending on locale. Homeowners also engage the sun's help in heating indoor and outdoor swimming pools. If built with the sun in mind and oriented optimally, many home designs can be adapted to take advantage of passive solar heating—or with solar avoidance as the primary focus in warmer climates.

Solar power generation has mainly been considered too expensive for anything but remote or portable applications, such as at cabins, on boats, or in recreational vehicles. However, the continual reduction in the price of solar panels and the introduction of new, more easily installed products may persuade more homeowners to look toward the sun as a competitive source of electrical power.

Storage and buyback

One of the hurdles to the development of alternative sources of energy has been the issue of storage of generated power. In a home setting, large banks of storage batteries take up space and need to be maintained. Plus they need replacement when their capacity to store power has been exhausted. But the willingness of utility companies to purchase power from individuals with excess power-generating capacity might spur further investment in alternative power systems. The ability to hook up to the grid to tap power when needed and to sell power back to the utility company when possible eliminates the necessity for on-site storage of power and its attendant space, maintenance, and cost problems. Utility companies also benefit from such arrangements. Any electricity they purchase from individuals is electricity they don't have to generate, which might give them the option to forestall building and maintaining additional power plants in the future.

Alternative heating and cooling sources

Most of the information in this book has focused on reducing energy consumption by changing habits and lifestyle and upgrading the energy efficiency of your home and everything in it. There are also ways to save energy that require investments in auxiliary heating or cooling equipment. These include the use of wood and corn stoves and swamp coolers for hot and arid climates.

Wood—a renewable fuel

Wood, of course, has been used as a heating fuel for as long as people have been on the earth. In the overall span of that time, only relatively recently have people sought to increase the benefit of wood's heat-producing ability by containing the burning process inside a metal enclosure. A variety of high-efficiency wood-burning stoves, fireplaces, and fireplace inserts are currently on the market.

Wood can be used as a primary heat source but more often plays a supplementary role to a central heating furnace or boiler. And while burning wood can reduce our dependence on oil or gas, the fact remains that wood has to come from somewhere. You have to purchase it or cut it, split it, stack it, and store it yourself. But for those with access to an inexpensive or free supply of wood, installing and using a wood-burning stove or insert can make a dramatic difference in your utility bill.

Fireplaces—not so efficient

Burning wood in an older, conventional fireplace is not the best way to generate heat; the wood burns uncontrollably and inefficiently. In fact, 90 percent of the heat energy produced goes up the flue, along with a lot of dirty smoke. Worse, this type of fire gobbles up a huge amount of room air that is used to help combust the fuel and convey it up the chimney. That air is drawn into the house from many different places: It leaks through and around windows and doors, and cracks and gaps in the exterior siding and foundation. It is possible to sit in a room that has a roaring fire blazing in an open fireplace, yet still feel a cold draft of air at your back as air rushes toward the fire.

Glass doors on the front of an open fireplace help increase the efficiency, but there is still a lot of heat going up the flue that could better be used to heat the house.

Fireplace inserts

A cast iron or steel fireplace insert mounted inside an open fireplace provides many of the benefits of a wood-burning stove. The metal radiates heat into the room, an adjustable opening on the front of the insert allows control of the air going into the firebox for more efficient burning, and many inserts are available with glass panels in the doors, which provide a view of the fire. Nearly any open fireplace can be retrofitted with an insert, and the difference in the heat produced is well worth the effort and expense.

Woodstoves

Cast-iron, steel, or stone woodstoves can be both beautiful and efficient. Like fireplace inserts, the metal radiates heat in all directions, the burning of the fire is controlled by regulating the flow of air into the firebox, and many stoves come with glass panels that allow the fire to be seen. A surround made of masonry material can soak up heat while the fire is burning and later radiate it into the house, acting as a heat-storage device.

A drawback to woodstoves is that they take up space in the home and might not be easily added to an existing home. A metal or masonry flue has to be provided for safe venting of the hot combustion gases, so a clear path from the stove to the roof has to be available. Additionally, as with any wood-burning device, hauling wood in and out during the heating season can be messy and might introduce insects into the home.

Stand-alone wood furnaces

Exterior wood furnaces hit the market some years ago, and their popularity continues to rise. A stand-alone unit consists of a small building outside the house that contains a large wood-burning stove. The stove heats a jacket filled with water, which is then pumped into the house through a set of underground pipes. The pipes enter the house and travel to a conventional air handler inside a furnace.

Inside the furnace the water passes through a heat exchanger unit that acts and looks much like the radiator on the front of a car. Water flowing through the heat exchanger gives up its heat to the air, pushed by the blower fan in the furnace. The heat is then distributed throughout the house through the existing ductwork.

The advantages to such systems are many. They require fueling only once or twice a day and burn large logs that don't require much splitting or cutting. The combustion process takes place safely outside the home. And the mess of hauling, splitting, and storing wood is all confined to the outdoors. The only thing that enters the house from the system is the hot water traveling through the piping. Provided with a source of wood for the winter, a homeowner could heat his or her entire home with such a system instead of just a room or two, as is typical with a woodstove or insert. If retrofitted to an existing HVAC system, the original gas or oil burner can be left in place, providing a convenient backup if, for instance, the occupants are away for several days.

Corn and pellet stoves

In areas where field corn, usually used to feed livestock, is available inexpensively, corn stoves are another heating alternative. Corn stoves have a hopper on top or on the side into which bags or bushels of loose corn are deposited. A thermostatically controlled auger shuffles kernels of the corn into a small firebox a few at a time. Inside the firebox a clean, intense fire combusts the corn, turning it into heat that is moved around the room by a small fan.

Homeowners with access to a small field and the means to plant and harvest their own corn or access to inexpensive corn purchased directly from a farmer or grain elevator can generate their own heat economically with a corn stove. Venting the stove can be accomplished via a small fluepipe that can either penetrate the roof or exit through a sidewall of the house. The latter feature can make the installation of a corn stove easier than a woodstove, in some cases.

Bags of corn can be stored in a compact space, can be hauled easily, and don't require any further processing—unlike the cutting and splitting necessary with wood. Because corn contains oil and ethanol, both of which burn cleanly, only a small amount of ash develops in the firebox. Some corn stoves draw combustion air from outside the house, eliminating the need for make-up air that otherwise would be drawn inside through holes and gaps in the building's exterior shell.

Corn stoves require electricity to operate and thus cannot run during a power outage. However, some have provisions for a backup battery that allows the stove to function in emergencies.

Some corn stoves can also burn pellets—compressed nuggets of sawmill waste. There are also pellet stoves available, designed only for that use. Corn cannot be burned in pellet stoves. Pellets are available in bags from farm and feed stores, as well as from places that sell wood and pellet stoves. Pellet and corn stoves are also available in fireplace insert configurations.

Masonry heaters

Unlike open fireplaces, masonry heaters burn wood in an enclosed firebox. The combustion gases travel through a maze of masonry passages where they release their heat. After the fire burns out, heat continues to radiate from the masonry for hours.

Masonry heaters are often large and expensive, and some of the ones made with polished soapstone are architectural marvels. Most masonry heaters are built into new homes since placing a foundation under one in an existing home can be problematic. Because of its size, a room or an entire area usually must be designed around a masonry heater.

While many woodstoves restrict the air intake in order to make wood burn longer, masonry heaters are made to accommodate short, hot fires. The heat extracted from the wood is then transferred to the masonry, which then releases that stored heat to the house after the fire goes out.

Swamp coolers

What if someone offered you the opportunity to purchase a device that would function similarly to an air conditioner at about half the price of a conventional A/C system and would run on a fraction of the electricity? Such a product exists. It's called a "swamp cooler" or "evaporative cooler."

Swamp coolers are designed to be used only in areas where the air is relatively dry, because they add moisture to the air. But in suitable climates, swamp coolers can reduce cooling costs dramatically.

In addition to lower initial costs, swamp coolers operate on less than a quarter of the electricity required by a conventional air-conditioning system. And they run on only 120 volts as opposed to 240 volts, which can cut installation costs further by eliminating the necessity for additional wiring or a possible electrical service upgrade.

Swamp coolers operate by blowing air through wet pads. The air emerges as much as 20 degrees cooler after it passes through the unit. Because particles of air pollutants

remain behind on the wet surface of the pads, swamp coolers provide some air filtration as well.

The air is blown into the house, slightly humidified. At least one window must be open when using a swamp cooler in order to allow the air to be blown inside to escape somewhere. There are some window-mounted swamp coolers available, but the usual installation is a whole-house system that can tie into existing or new ductwork. Water can be supplied manually to a holding tank or automatically via a hose or piped connection; consumption averages between about 2–15 gallons per day. Systems can use a thermostat for control purposes, and 2- or 3-stage or variable-speed fans provide precise management of the cool air input.

Maintenance consists of replacing the pads periodically and cleaning the unit. Pad longevity can be extended by ensuring the water sprayed on or dripped through the pads is of good quality. Hard-water minerals can build up on the pads and reduce their capacity for evaporation, thus diminishing the efficiency of the device.

SAVING MONEY AND ENERGY

We live in age when energy has elevated the quality of our lives to a level undreamed of by our ancestors. In every aspect of our lives energy plays a significant role. Whether we are on the move in our vehicles or reclining in our homes, energy is being used to power our transportation or to keep us comfortable. But just because that energy is

so accessible that does not mean that we need not be good stewards of nature's gift to us.

By implementing many of the suggestions in this energy guide, you will be saving considerable money, and equally important, you will be conserving energy for future generations. Thus, we can look back to realize how fortunate we are to live in today's world and at the same time envision a future in which our natural resources are still abundantly available for our children and our children's children.